W0232760

PENGUIN BOOKS
DIDDI

Ira Pande worked as a university teacher for fifteen years, and then as an editor at *Seminar*, *Biblio*, Dorling Kindersley and Roli Books. She has done some work for television and has also acted in the award-winning film *Monsoon Wedding*. Currently, she works a freelance writer and editor.

DIDDI

My Mother's Voice

IRA PANDE

PENGUIN BOOKS

An imprint of Penguin Random House

PENGUIN BOOKS

USA | Canada | UK | Ireland | Australia
New Zealand | India | South Africa | China | Singapore

Penguin Books is part of the Penguin Random House group of companies
whose addresses can be found at global.penguinrandomhouse.com

Published by Penguin Random House India Pvt. Ltd
4th Floor, Capital Tower 1, MG Road,
Gurugram 122 002, Haryana, India

Penguin
Random House
India

First published by Penguin Books India 2005

12 11 10 9 8 7 6 5

ISBN 9780143033462

Typeset in Aldine401 BT by R. Ajith Kumar, New Delhi

Printed at Repro India Limited

www.penguin.co.in

MIX
Paper from
responsible sources
FSC® C047271

This is a legitimate digitally printed version of the book and therefore might not
have certain extra finishing on the cover.

For Jiya

Contents

Acknowledgements   viii

Prologue   1

1   Diddi's Kasoon   8

2   Ama   39

3   Santiniketan   56

4   Diddi and Babu   68

5   Priory Lodge   88

6   Binu   104

7   Jayanti Jerja   118

8   Hamid Bhai   137

9   Ramrati   153

10   The Last Chapter   175

Epilogue: Pootonwali   185

Acknowledgements

In February 2004, my mother-in-law, Jiya, was diagnosed with cancer of the tongue. Jiya, to whom I dedicate this book, was never a mother-in-law: she was my best friend. I wrote this book whenever I could snatch time in those painful months when we all suffered with her and finished the first draft in four months, so that she could read it while she had the energy to. She did, and then wrote on a slate (she could not speak clearly then), 'I give you the Nobel Prize for this.' For her faith in me and the love she gave me so generously, I dedicate this book to her, someone who was more a mother to me than my own.

There are some special friends who helped me carry on writing even when it was difficult to find the will or time. Dipa Chaudhuri, Sanjeev Saith, Alok Rai, Pankaj Butalia, Shobha Dev, Abhinav Dhar, Meera Malik are among those few friends to whom I showed a draft of this book and who gave me wonderful feedback. Anuradha Roy, who first set me off by commissioning an article on Diddi for the *Hindu*, is someone I owe a lunch of gratitude. V.K. Karthika, Jaishree Ram Mohan and Bena Sarin of Penguin have been a dream team, and produced this book in record time. I thank them all.

My sisters and brother allowed me to do whatever I wanted to with Diddi's books and actually helped me locate some missing articles and stories. Without their support, I would have never dared to write.

My children, Apurva-Chinmaya, Aditya and Aftab, have been enthusiastic readers and been a part of this whole venture. Aditya, who designed the cover, was with me throughout the writing of the book and even fibbed to make the right noises. But it is to Amitabha, my husband (long-suffering, patient and wise), that I owe more than a debt. It is he who helped me to think towards writing this book with Diddi as a character in her own world, and not as a memoir that I had originally planned. Many arguments and tantrums from me were borne with his characteristic fortitude. Without him there, I would never have completed this book or given it to a publisher.

~
_____

Prologue

Perhaps because we called our mother Diddi, elder sister, our relationship with her was always somewhat ambivalent. More than a mother she was for us a difficult sibling, an eccentric, much older sister who belonged to a different generation. After her death, it seemed to me as if she had lodged herself in my head because I could hear her voice constantly, more clearly than I ever heard her when she was alive. It occurred to me then that despite the fact that she was never a cloying presence, she had burrowed herself so deeply into my life that losing her was like losing a limb. Or perhaps it was something like the phenomenon that people with amputated limbs describe when they can feel sensations in an arm or leg that is no longer there.

That she was also the most popular Hindi writer of her times was an aspect of her personality that we were both proud of and embarrassed by. She was too proud to mention how hurt she was by my casual acceptance of her literary reputation. It must have pained her deeply that the very children who had once never tired of hearing her fascinating stories had now outgrown her kind of writing. So she chose to deliberately downplay her literary reputation with us, treating it as a joke that she got hundreds of letters and awards from many sources. Making fun of one's achievements was a game we had learnt to play from her and understood, so we played along.

This was one of the reasons that after her death in March 2003, I vowed to read all her works again, many of which, I'm ashamed to admit, I had never read at all. While reading her prose writings it dawned on me that over the same half century that she wrote her most popular novels and short stories, she had also published a large body of autobiographical prose. And that it is primarily in her non-fiction—her portraits, essays, memoirs, chronicles, travelogues and newspaper columns—that she kept a kind of personal record of her life. As I read them, some remembered as stories she had told us as children, others I remembered reading when they were first written, it became clear to me that until I absorbed *this* part of her work, and the personality embedded there, she would never move out of my head.

This book is not meant to be anything as literary as a biography. Indeed, while writing it I deliberately put aside all that I ever learnt as an editor. For the more I read her and tried to recreate her voice, the more I became involved in a psyche and a temperament that used the senses as well as the mind rather than the mere intellect. I do not know whether Diddi herself necessarily understood, or intended to understand, this aspect of her work, for like so many writers, she could embody truth, but did not always know it. Or if she did, she chose to hide it.

In this sense, I suppose, every writer becomes a character in the fictional world he or she creates. I can't say whether this is a universal truth, but I do know that Diddi bled into her plots often without knowing that she was doing so. I suspect this was her way of marking a place for herself in everything she created so that her voice would never be stilled or forgotten by anyone who had heard it. In the same way that she left a bit of herself in each of her children, she left bits of herself in every piece she wrote. Doubtless, there are several writers and artists who, like her, cannot bear to be excluded from the world that they create. Diddi created her fictional universe from the part of her life she loved best: her childhood and early years. Time and again, she used Kumaon and Bengal as the setting for her romantic novels and she clung to these territories as a child to a mother's hand. They gave her the strength to face the encounters, people and places she feared to confront. A part of her, I am convinced, always stood at the top of her childhood home and looked down confidently at the passers-by on the road below, secure in the knowledge that she had something that none of them even *knew*.

Her writings of her childhood are a marvellous mixture of memory and fiction, a fact that becomes evident as the reader discovers that she uses an event in a portrait of a real person and then again as a situation or character in a novel. She looked and treated all of us as characters she used and controlled. And to liberate herself from the frustration when she—like all romantic dreamers—encountered the complexities of real lives, real people. I also know now that despite her lofty proclamations of detachment, she could never bear to let go of us. So when we all moved away, she remembered us as characters so that she could always keep us near her in the only way she knew— through her writing.

Yet she also knew—perhaps the word is trusted—that to be born sentient and watchful is a daily miracle; that the world around us is as wondrous an index of heaven as we shall ever know; that to abide here is the nearest you can get to heaven because it is a chance to watch and take part in so many lives. Entering other people's homes and lives gave her the best chance to find a better and better image with which to secure it for her readers. For a person as restless and alive as she was, one life, one pair of eyes, one heart was not enough. Perhaps this is why after she lost us to our own lives and families, she created another family for herself in Lucknow and ruled over them like a queen. My sister Mrinal—the child nearest to her own restless temperament—called her Queen Lear because she always travelled with her personal fool. Her maid, Ramrati, was Diddi's alter ego, and her family and friends became Diddi's Lucknow court. Among the regular visitors to this world were the local hijra, Mohabbat, the milkman, Suleiman, the vegetable vendor, the postman, and Qutb Ali, her faithful rickshawallah. An occasional visitor was a monkey (named Ramkali) who used to wear her glasses and 'read' the newspapers with her in the morning, or so she said. This was the court that she presided over and that supplied her with all the stories that came tumbling out of her.

One of her greatest qualities was her capacity to befriend people of whatever class and creed and especially those who would be intellectually and socially unacceptable to most of us. It was this endearing lack of conceit that made her a bit of an embarrassment to her own children. Yet Diddi was also a fearful snob—an intellectual snob—and was instinctively drawn to the pure of spirit. It was this that won her the fierce loyalty of whoever she had around her. In her tribute to Ramrati, she writes:

My Guru, Acharya Hajari Prasad Dwivedi, once said in a lecture, 'The common people you have around you are a treasure. Remember that they represent a rich cultural tradition: make them the subject of your study. Look closely at the people you work with, observe their language, thoughts, their social units, their lifestyles and beliefs. You will learn more from them than from hours spent in a library or museum. Yet remember that you must interact with them in a responsible manner: do all you can to make them understand their past, see their present for what it is and prepare them to face their future. In short, learn from them and teach them.'

I have no doubt at all that no lecture in the world can better the lessons given by life and the ordinary people around us. I have met some outstanding minds and learnt valuable lessons from them. My teachers came in many shapes and forms and what they taught me has helped me immeasurably in negotiating the difficulties I have faced.

So let me begin with Almora, where it all starts.

I remember *my* father's house in the cantonment area where we lived until I was three years old. All I can remember is that it had a red tin roof, a little garden pavilion and a hen coop. Magnificent deodar trees shielded it from the gaze of the Circuit House on top of the hill and far below us lay Almora's Lala Bazaar with its quaint cobbled lanes and sleepy shops. Yet more than the details of the house it is smells and sounds that I remember: the sound of the wind rustling through the deodars and the warm smell of crushed pine needles, the drone of fat bumblebees in the summer and the lonely cawing of the crows in winter.

However, since we spent most of our time at the other end of town, in my grandmother's house at Kasoon, *that* is the house that I remember with a Fellini-like vividness. It was perched on a ridge that offered a sweeping view of virtually the whole town. I remember its stone flagged courtyard, its long wooden veranda that overlooked the street below and a trapdoor that separated the top storey from the ground floor and led directly to the passage adjoining the library. Ama, my grandmother, was a plump, bespectacled and toothless presence who presided over an empire of pretty unmarried daughters, grandchildren and hangers-on from the past. She seldom moved from her rooms on the upper floor and loved my uncle Tribhi's children more than the rest of us put together. Yet, in the innocent way that children store happy memories, I have no recollection of being jealous of the fact that my uncle Tribhi and his family were placed on a level that none of us would ever reach.

According to the peculiar social dynamics of the Almora of those days your social position was determined neither by your wealth nor by your station in life. It was fundamentally attached to your birth and to the clan you belonged. If I were to draw a map of Almora from memory, it would be a sea of islands named after families and family homes: Champa Naula, Bishtakura, Jhijhar, Sela Khola, Tyunara, Dhunga Dhara, Pande Khola, Jivanpur, Galli, Malla Kasoon, Talla Kasoon. These were the fortresses of old Brahmin families who married eternally among themselves. Little wonder that madness mushroomed happily in the town and each clan had its share of lunatics.

In fact, one entire branch of my mother's family was cheerfully acknowledged as the mad people of Talla Kasoon. Ama said an ancestor of theirs had killed one of their farm hands. The father of the dead man cursed his landlord saying, 'May not even a calf ever prosper in your house!' And truly, no one in that house was normal or prosperous. Two of them, Bhagwat Da and Mohan Da, were amiable lunatics who often sauntered over to visit Kasoon. We touched Bhagwat Da's feet as we would touch those of any elder uncle when he strode across the courtyard to visit Ama. Dressed in rags and feathers, he held a staff festooned with flags and came to play a solitary game of table tennis downstairs in the library. He would chuck the ping-pong ball across the table and solemnly say, 'One love,' then cross over to the other side to toss the ball across to make it 'One all'. When he had played enough, he went upstairs to chat with my grandmother and drink a glass of tea with her. His wife was a schoolteacher who worked hard to keep the family going and once came to my father, then in the Education Department, to plead for a transfer from Almora. Apparently, Bhagwat Da had taken to attending her classes to the delight of the students. He held up his hand to answer every question she asked the class and even participated in the annual sports day races.

Across the terraced field lived the family of Mayaram Da, once my grandfather's driver and now part of my uncle Tribhi's staff. He called Tribhi Mama 'Highness' and smelt of cigarettes and sycophancy. In what was once the cowshed, lived Tara Didi, Ama's faithful Sancho Panza. A contractor in Burma, Tara Didi's husband died suddenly, leaving her alone and virtually destitute in a foreign land. How she found her way back to Almora is another story but she and her children were adopted by Ama and she remained Ama's faithful companion to the end. Tara Didi's kitchen smelt of warm chapattis and generosity.

In contrast was our own house in the cantonment: my father disliked noise and loud laughter. And he disapproved of Diddi's constant visits to Kasoon. I don't think he understood or wanted to acknowledge Diddi's deep attachment to her childhood home and its lively, noisy people. If I were Fellini and this was a film script, I would bathe Kasoon in bright sunshine and the cantonment house in a dark, brooding sadness. But to understand Diddi's love of Kasoon and its loony inmates, one has to read her own version of it.

1

Diddi's Kasoon

These reminiscences are taken from a selection Diddi's writing in the sixties/seventies, mainly from an article she wrote on Lohaniji when he died.

My earliest memories of Lohaniji are from the time we were in Gujarat, in Verawal. Lohaniji took us every morning to the Somnath temple and then let us play nearby as he lay under a tree to sing hymns to the Devi. His favourite was an invocation to the Devi who rides a tiger and his deep baritone would occasionally draw a passing shepherd as an audience. 'I have a feeling the old man knows only one song,' my brother once said deliberately within his hearing. 'Otherwise why would he sing a hymn to the Devi in a temple for Shiva?'

'Oh ho,' roared Lohaniji. 'You think I don't know any hymns to Shiva? Then listen to this one, you fools!' and he launched into a thrilling Shiva *stotra*. When he came to *Dhagadh-dhagadh dhagjjval lalaat patt pavake*, we stopped breathing as Lohaniji's voice thundered like a train across the windswept field.

His real name was Purushottam (literally, the best of men) Lohani and it was a name he lived up to. Tall, fair, with a bushy moustache bristling under a sharp, patrician nose, Lohaniji had large eyes and lips that rarely smiled. He was fond of reminding us that he had come into the family a year before my mother came to Kasoon as a bride. This is why even after she became a grandmother, he always referred to my mother as Dhulaini-jyu (bride).

Lohaniji was originally appointed to take charge of our kitchen but gradually all the important portfolios of the house came under his control. He handed over the task of cooking to his younger brother, Devidutt, and became instead the home, finance, information and broadcasting minister all rolled in one. In addition to this, he was the Chief of Protocol in my grandfather's household. Distinguished visitors—Tagore, Pandit Madan Mohan Malviya, Swami Nityanand, Sir Girija Shankar Bajpai, Sir Sultan Ahmad, Dr Ansari, the wrestler Rammurthi, and various royal guests, such as the Nawab of Rampur, Murtaza Ali Khan, would regularly come to Almora and often stay in our house. The Crown Prince of Datia, nicknamed Bulbul, stayed for over a year as our house guest. My father told us that his stepmother had tried to poison the prince and he had been sent to Almora for safety with my father as his guardian. Traumatized by his childhood memories of Datia, Bulbul would jump at unexpected sounds and crept around the house like a shadow behind my father.

Lohaniji was also our unofficial family priest: the long morning and evening puja, the rudri path at the annual Parthiv Puja in the rainy season, birthdays, deaths—Lohaniji oversaw the conduct of all these rituals. His own family—two sons, one daughter and a son-in-law, and his 'Bamini', a wife he loved deeply—were second to ours and he visited them once a year. For the rest of the year, he forgot he had any other family but us.

The four oldest children of our large family of siblings were especially close to him. Lohaniji had declared my eldest sister Chanda, who died at a tragically young age, a divine soul. She was not destined to stay in this sinful world for long, he'd say, shaking his head sadly. She was his favourite, a dev kanya: he had cradled her when she was born and she died with her head in his lap. My handsome brother, Tribhuvan, was born after two sisters and was the eldest son of the family. Lohaniji, an unashamed sexist, loved him dearly. Tribhi was allowed liberties no one else could take and called him Parkhiya, an affectionate swear word.

My father was Lalsaip, a Lohani-ized version of Lalla sahib (beloved son). 'One mistake Lalsaip has made, and which he will rue later,' he'd announce for all to hear, 'is entrusting the education of his eldest son to those monkey-faced white women. Just see how wild he has become already! Arrey, what do you expect of people who wipe their bums with paper!' He spat here to show his disgust for people who did not wash their bottoms with water. 'They've already changed his name, now they'll work on his mind!'

Tribhuvan was sent by my father to live in a cottage in Nainital with an English governess, Mrs Mumford, and her daughter, who gave him a new name—Tikker. When he came home, Lohaniji almost burst a blood vessel as he reported, 'He is asking for a knife and fork to eat his chapattis with! I'm warning you, Dhulaini-jyu,' he spluttered, 'the time has come to put a sacred thread round his neck, and get him away from the evil influence of those two witches.'

His impassioned appeal led to my brother's sacred thread ceremony that winter. We were in Orchcha, where my father was the Dewan, and the event was nothing short of a wedding, I tell you. Our clan priest, Tikaramji, brought a contingent of pandits from Banaras. Maharaja Birju Sinhdeo's royal elephant caparisoned with gold and silver ornaments stood at the gates of our house, decked like a bride. Lohaniji was called to whisper the sacred mantra in my brother's ears and he hissed, 'You are Tribhuvan once more, now, do you hear? No one will call you Tikker ever again!'

It was perhaps on Lohaniji's pleading that our education underwent a radical shift. We three, Jayanti, Tribhi and I, were packed off to my grandfather's home in Almora and Lohaniji became our guardian. Pandit Gangadutt taught us Sanskrit; our mathematics teacher was Raghuvar Datt Joshi, widely regarded as the Ramanujan of Kumaon; while our grandfather himself took on the responsibility of teaching us English and Hindi.

Lohaniji would shake us awake at five in the morning. He watched as we splashed our faces with cold water, bathed our eyes with Triphala and then herded us off on a long walk (Tribhi called it a safari). On our return, we were handed a glass of hot milk and Lohaniji would settle down to his long puja. I can taste that delicious milk even now, laced with ground almonds and crushed cardamoms and sweetened with sugar. Lohaniji used to get the rich milk from a special village, Phalsima, famous for its milk and dairy products. The head milkman there, Nagmal, was bullied to pulp by Lohaniji to ensure that he never dared to water it down.

'Look here, Nagmaliya, you worm, if you ever dare to add even a drop of water to the milk you bring to this house, I'll burn you to a cinder with my Brahmin eye.'

'How can you even think of such a thing, Guru,' the poor man stammered. 'Add water in the milk for this house? I don't want to go to hell, Ram, Ram…'

Lohaniji had terrorized not just poor Nagmal and all the servants of the house but the town's shopkeepers and vendors as well. He had told them all that his Guru, the awesome Narad Baba, had taught him ways of punishing human beings that they couldn't dream of. According to Lohaniji, Narad Baba had taught him several secret mantras: among them was the art of getting stoned. Smoking marijuana was Lohaniji's only vice and often, when lighting up his chillum, he would roll his red eyes to say:

Better a girl than a boy
Who has not tasted pot!

All we knew was that as soon as he took his first puff, his mood changed magically for the better.

Every morning, before we joined our grandfather for our lessons in the library downstairs, Lohaniji would make us write these lines from the great poet Tulsidas:

Patience, faith and a discerning mind
These are true companions in dark times.
Literature, courage, honesty and God, says Tulsidas,
Will never let you down.

Day after day he made us transcribe them a hundred times to improve our handwriting. 'Don't you know any other lines, Lohaniji?' we occasionally whined. One silent look from him at his puja and we would go back wearily to our task. I realize now that even though we did not understand their meaning and considered the daily grind some kind of Chinese torture he inflicted on us, Lohaniji embedded them so firmly in our minds and hearts that they became a sort of touchstone in our lives.

~

The house adjoining my grandfather's belonged to the family of Daniel Pant, a Christian who was once related to us from my mother's family. However, after Daniel Pant converted to Christianity, our orthodox grandfather erected a wall to separate their world from ours so that we had nothing to do with each other. The three of us were sternly forbidden to even look that way.

The wall may have separated our two homes but our worlds constantly collided. Right next to the wall lay their kitchen, and maddening aromas of delicious meats being cooked in their house wafted over, sneaked across to our boring Brahmin kitchen to inflict a resounding defeat on the pathetic dal, potato curry and rice that Devidutt dished up day after day. Knowing what that tempting aroma did to our Brahmin souls, Lohaniji would immediately shut the windows of our kitchen against its polluting intrusion, muttering curses under his breath as he did so. Sadly for him, it snaked its way through the cracks in the wooden shutters and doors and continued to drive us mad.

We knew the children on the other side of our Berlin Wall—partly because we were after all from the same stock but also because their free and open lifestyle was so different from ours that it appeared infinitely more appealing than our spartan Brahmin regimen. Of all the children on the other side of the wall, Henry Pant was my special friend. He wore shining leather shoes, striped socks and sparkling white shirts with starched collars and a smart tie. His sisters Olga and Muriel (whom we called Marial behind her back) would change into gossamer Bamberg georgette saris in the evening for their customary stroll to the market. We almost died of envy.

'Lucky bums!' Tribhi sighed one day. 'Look at the life they have and look at us! We have *Pilgrim's Progress* and the *Amar Kosh* stuffed down our throats while they get to do whatever they want. Do you know,' he told me, envy dripping from every syllable, 'Henry eats an egg *every* day!'

'Really?'

'Yes! They also eat meat every day.'

Henry had draped himself over the wall and joined in the conversation at this point. 'Not just every day, at every meal,' he sprinkled salt on our wounds. 'Not like you Hindus who eat greens and roots all the time!' he added pityingly.

'You may have forgotten that your grandfather and mine were first cousins, Henry Pant,' I spat back, 'we haven't. *He* must have eaten the same greens and roots once.' Henry was forced to concede this round to me and perhaps as a concession to the important historical issue I had raised offered us deprived vegetarians a deal.

'If you are dying to see what we eat, I can arrange it,' he said loftily. 'But no one must ever get to know.' Tribhi and I had our tongues hanging out by now and looked at him hopefully. Henry slid a hand into the pocket of his shorts, and drew himself up. 'The price will be four walnuts each from the tree in your garden. At exactly ten every morning our cook puts the meat into the pot in our courtyard. If you can swing yourselves up that pomegranate tree there, and manage to perch on the wall, I'll take care of the rest. We have a ladder on the other side and I'll help you down to our side of the house.' Then, like the Cheshire Cat, he disappeared from view but not before he reminded us of the rates of exchange: four walnuts from our tree for one sniff of their divine meat curry. His generous offer set our hearts aflutter: we could hardly imagine what the real curry would be like, when its mere aroma wafting through Lohaniji's barricaded kitchen maddened us.

On the dot of ten, the familiar fragrance wafted over. We rose to the call of the bubbling pot on the other side, furtively collected the mandatory eight walnuts and crawled across the sliding roof of my uncle's house to reach the pomegranate tree. We knew that its branches were very frail, yet we swung ourselves from there, egged on by the tempting aroma of the ambrosial meat pot that got stronger with each step. We stood trembling on the wall. Below us was Henry. 'Have you brought the walnuts?' he asked first.

'Yes.'

He whipped out the ladder and helped us down. There in front of us was a coal angeethi and on top of it was the pot of meat, bubbling away merrily. For a long while, we just gazed in ecstasy at the spectacle. Our hearts rose and fell with each rise and fall of the lid.

'Give me the walnuts,' commanded Henry.

I quickly handed over the tax.

'Remember you can smell it only once,' he reminded me. 'Four walnuts earn just one sniff.'

I nodded. He lifted the lid and I shut my eyes to inhale the smell deep into my soul.

A few years later, we went back from Almora to our parents. My father moved from one princely state to another as a Dewan and our lives underwent a dramatic change. We now lived a life of epicurean bliss compared to our days in Almora. There was not a single living thing we did not taste—waterbirds of all sizes and shapes, sambar, wild geese, turkey, turtles, partridges and quails, you name it. In Rampur, where my father was the Home Minister to the Nawab, every day a specially sealed dastarkhan would arrive from the royal kitchen. Before the Nawab ate anything, it had to be certified fit for the royal palate by my father. Then the meal was sealed once more and sent back. Often, we used to sneak a morsel from the platter.

But I tell you even then nothing ever matched the pure bliss of the sniff of Henry's meat pot in Almora.

~

Those were the golden years of our life. Our house had a huge staff—Sohan Singh, Bishan Singh, Ummaid Singh, Thul (Big) Gusain and his brother Nan (Small) Gusain. Thul Gusain was the oldest of them all and a man of rather refined tastes. He was tall, with a long nose and wore little gold studs in his ears. My father was now Home Minister to the Nawab of Rampur and Lohaniji, who had seen diamond studs in the Nawab's ears, used to sarcastically call Thul Gusain the Nawab of Anyarkot (the dark land), because his village lay close to the cremation grounds. Lohaniji declared that the smoke from the pyres had gone to Gusain's head and fogged his brain. 'That's why it takes his brain so long to follow instructions,' he was fond of saying. Nevertheless, he was quite partial to Thul Gusain. Then, suddenly, Lohaniji began to call him a 'masaniya' (a low-caste man who stokes funeral pyres). 'Tell that masaniya to set the curds,' he would tell another servant. Or, 'Tell the masaniya to pick up the clothes from the terrace—it looks like it's going to pour any minute.' We were a little puzzled at Thul Gusain's sudden demotion from nawab to masaniya.

Then one day, it all became clear. 'Don't dare think, masaniya,' Lohaniji was telling Thul Gusain, 'that I have only two eyes. I have two at the back of my head as well, understand?'

'Why do you say that, Guru? What did you see?' Gusain stuttered, nursing the red weal from the slap that Lohaniji had just planted on his cheek.

Lohaniji drew himself to his full height and thundered, 'You dare to ask me that? Do you have any concern for the name and reputation of this house? Go slog somewhere else if this is how you want to behave. You are the father of two children, you shameless wretch, and your daughter is married to Nagmal's son. Did you ever stop to think what will happen to her if her father-in-law finds out?'

Thul Gusain bowed his head in shame as Lohaniji ranted. Later, we heard that Gusain had been spotted by Lohaniji flirting in the dark lane behind our house with a low-caste girl. Apparently he had hoped to marry her secretly.

That day, we saw Gusain place his cap at Lohaniji's feet and beg for forgiveness. But Lohaniji would not be moved. 'Had you stolen money or gold, I may have forgiven you. But immoral behaviour I will not condone.'

My mother pleaded his case but Lohaniji refused to melt. He dismissed Thul Gusain and none of us asked why he could not be given another chance.

In those days, girls and women from high-born Brahmin families were not allowed to go to the market. There were just two occasions in the year when this rule was relaxed: the day of the Nanda Devi fair and on Diwali. Even then, we were allowed to watch the procession only from the balcony of Badrilal Sah's house. Sahji was my grandfather's friend and his house with its beautifully carved doors and balcony was a great vantage point. However, Lohaniji occasionally took me, the baby of the family, to the market with him. The beginning and end of such an expedition was the shop of his buddy, Sundarlal Sah. His smooth fair face with a sandalwood tilak on his forehead used to light up when he spotted Lohaniji. 'Come, come, Guru,' he would greet his friend. 'So, what's happening?'

And the two would swap gossip and news. Tired of their inane conversation and with my head reeling from the sickening odour of the Himalayan herbs and spices—jambu, gandhrain—sold in Sundarlal Sah's grocery store, I would get restive. Lohaniji would pass me a bit of churan or some bulls' eyes (whatever happened to those delightful sweets, I wonder?) to keep me quiet. Finally, I would start whining, 'Come on, Lohaniji, let's go to the bazaar, please!'

17

'Keep quiet, girl,' he'd snap back. 'What is this if not the bazaar? Girls should not go beyond this point. Haven't you heard me say: Woman must never go to the bazaar / And men never to the larder.'

But like all little girls I yearned to visit the flea market outside Ramsay School, where stalls sold fake coral necklaces, shining ornaments, bells, ribbons and trinkets that you braided into your plaits and swung around. What joy it was to swing your plait with those baubles on them! Sometimes I pity the children I see now, with their collection of electronic toys. They will never discover the joy that we held in the palm of our hands. Kite-flying, grinding glass to stick to the string, a trick my brother taught me, or tossing a pebble up in the air and sweeping the others on the ground before it landed in a game of gitti. The adroitness of manouevres like ikkam, dukkam, muththi—what do they know of these? What about kissing a stone for luck and tossing it across the stones before a game of hopscotch? All these are lost arts now and more's the pity.

The children of today tire of their toys because they have so many to choose from. On the other hand, no matter how often we played cat's cradle or sang the local version of 'Oranges and lemons', we never felt bored. My sister Jayanti's skill at making ragdolls was awesome and once, when, after a fight, my brother tossed my favourite ragdoll into the fire, I wept as if I had lost a child.

If ever one of us fell ill, Lohaniji was summoned to help. To ease an earache, he would rub the leaf of the madar plant between his palms and put two drops in the offending ear. The pain vanished. And I must tell you the secret of why none of us ever suffered from a stye in the eye.

One day, Lohaniji dragged a snake charmer to the house. We looked at his fearful red eyes, his matted locks and huge turquoise earrings hanging from lobes that touched his shoulders and almost ran inside. His beard was parted in two halves and dyed red with henna. From his shoulder hung a bamboo pole with a basket at each end. We could hear the hiss of the snakes that lay in there beneath the covers.

'Here, maharaj,' said the man and lifted his reed pipe to his mouth as he uncovered the basket. He started to play on the pipe and the snakes slowly emerged from their baskets. 'I have brought these beauties straight from Amarkantak. See, even their fangs have not been taken out!'

Then, to our horror, he lifted one of them and folded it like a posy. Lohaniji made us shut our eyes and the man touched the slithering snake to our closed eyes as he chanted some mantra. 'There!' he said in a satisfied tone. 'Now these children will never get a stye. I will shave off half my moustache if they do.'

Lohaniji was convinced this treatment would work and none of us dared to ask where we would find the magician if it failed and we needed to shave off his moustache. However, his snake guarded our eyes so well that we never ever suffered from a stye in the eye. Lohaniji's skill as a dentist was no less impressive. The minute a milk tooth was ready for pulling out, he would lasso it out with a piece of thread and make us bury it under a fresh patch of grass. As a special treat, we were given delicious semolina halwa dripping with ghee. We all had straight teeth and when I see little children with wires cruelly holding their teeth in, I feel the pain they have to undergo to be able to smile prettily when they grow up. Perhaps people today have ceased to believe in the natural processes of growth and natural correctives. Everyone wants to be perfect, look perfect and suffer for it.

Lohaniji's repertoire of ghost stories was legendary and he claimed each one was true.

'I don't know why these damned female spirits like me,'

Lohaniji told us. 'The minute I walk past a peepal tree, they fall into my lap like raindrops! But not one of them,' he declared proudly, 'has succeeded in casting a spell on me.'

His favourite story was called *Jago ho! Main le unyuin* (Wait for me!). It was set at midnight, the witching hour of the hills. Lohaniji was returning from his village and walking past a cremation ground, when a khabees (a male spirit with red eyes) started to dog his steps. Every time Lohaniji turned round, the khabees would change into a bull, or a hissing snake, or a dhobi and call out, *Jago ho! Main le unyuin*. At this point, Lohaniji would imitate that nasal *Jago ho!* elongating the sound of the *ho* to send a shiver down our spines. We would scream in terror and beg him to stop. Lohaniji would roar with laughter and say, 'Stupid children, no spirit can come near this house as long as I am around.'

Truly, his departure from our house brought all the evil spirits out of the walls. Death, disease, penury—these were the evil spirits Lohaniji had valiantly kept at bay.

In those days, our house had two libraries: one was my grandfather's and the other belonged to my mother. In contrast to my grandfather's collection, which was in the library downstairs, my mother's library had a vast range of fiction locked away in a wooden glass-fronted cupboard in the room adjoining the veranda upstairs. Bankimchandra, Premchand, Saratchandra, Meghani and all the popular writers in Bengali and Gujarati along with hundreds of Gujarati and Hindi magazines lined her bookshelves. We were a family of bookworms and spent hours devouring books hungrily, sprawled in the sun on the veranda with the sounds of the street filtering in like a pleasant record playing in the background.

In addition to this treasure, our supplies of reading matter came from a unique travelling library. A vendor arrived periodically with a huge trunk of second-hand books carried by a Nepali coolie. No book cost more than eight annas and often, because we were such avid readers, he would add a few for free. However, unlike the home library, his books were not the classics but pulp fiction and worse. I had heard others in the family speak of some famous pornography titles and one that took my fancy was called *Kissa Tota-Maina* (The tale of a parrot and a mynah). I spotted the forbidden title one day and looked around furtively before burying it among my pile of books. I had barely straightened up, when Lohaniji gave me a resounding slap across my face. My jaw almost dropped off and I heard him say, 'Have you not heard me tell you never to read such books?' I still remember that slap: it was almost as bad as the one I got from my mother when she caught me slyly reading *Saraswatichandra*, a forbidden Gujarati romance in her library.

Life dealt several unkind blows to Lohaniji over the years. He saw the death of my grandfather, whom he worshipped, then the rapid deaths of Chanda our eldest sister, my father and my uncle. Yet he stayed on, bending with each blow like an old banyan tree. The glory of a golden era ended when my father died and my mother was left with a large brood of children to bring up and no money. One by one, she pensioned off our servants. Then it was the turn of the monogrammed silver thalis and vessels to be discreetly hawked. Our carpets, my father's brocade sherwanis, his Banarasi turbans, his gold cufflinks and diamond buttons—all vanished one by one, leaving gaps and holes all over the house. Finally, my mother was forced to sell off the silver paandaan, with its dainty chains and boxes, which she had brought in her dowry. Lohaniji himself used to take charge of the paan ceremony, which entailed adding all the ingredients to tender betel leaves, and cutting the areca nuts and cloves and cardamoms. He would then string them from silver chains or place them on a silver salver for offering to my grandfather's guests. With the paandaan went the silver rose-water sprinklers as well. Lohaniji wrapped them all up in old rags one day and took them to the pawnbroker. When he returned, he stood against the wall of the courtyard in such a dejected way that we thought he had heard of a death in the bazaar.

Old age finally caught up with Lohaniji: his eyes became rheumy and clouded and he lost so much weight that his black bandgala coat hung loosely on his frame. This coat that he wore over a white cricket jersey my father had once brought him from England was his signature attire. Now his clothes began to look as if they were rags hung on some scarecrow. The only relic from the past that still ticked away was the pocket watch he wore. Its tick-tock had regulated the heartbeat of our home but now you could hardly hear it. Like so much else, it was slowly winding down.

Our only visitors now were the bearers of bills and bad news and Lohaniji used to scoff:

I've seen Pandes, I've seen Pants

Before I die, I suppose I have to see these.

The 'these' were the poor peasants from our village who came with pathetic offerings from our fields and the Pandes and Pants were other high-born Brahmins.

My mother often pleaded with Lohaniji to retire but he was determined to see my brother Tribhi married and to bring up his children. So naturally, when the time came for that, he was entrusted with the task of going to see the girl my mother had selected for Tribhi. You should have seen how he puffed out his chest and how his lips smiled through his bushy moustache as he made his way to my brother's fiancee's home. 'Who is this young man, then, Lohaniji?' we teased him as he fussed over his turban and coat.

As soon as we heard he'd returned, we all crowded round him. 'What is she like, Lohaniji?'

'Pure gold,' was his verdict.

We waited for him to elaborate, and then when he showed no signs of breaking the silence, one of us asked, 'Is she fair or not?'

'How do I know?' he countered. 'I didn't see her face!'

'What!' my sister asked. 'Then whose face did you go to see? Her mother's?'

'Yes,' he nodded. 'If you choose a girl, you must see her mother. I tell you, she must have a beautiful complexion and as for her manners! They must be perfect as well.'

'You mean you *really* did not see her face?' we persisted.

'No. I just saw her hands and nails as she sat with her head bowed near her mother.'

'This is what comes of sending an old fuddy-duddy like Lohaniji to see a girl,' we scolded our mother. 'Are we talking of a cow or a bride for this house?' Lohaniji would check an animal's hooves and decide whether it was fit or not.

'Quiet!' my mother thundered. 'Lohaniji lived with Narad Baba—what he doesn't know about human nature is not worth knowing!'

Finally, Lohaniji left one day to be with his beloved Bamini saying he wanted to spend his last days with her. We had seen her only rarely and remembered her as a shy, submissive thing. However, at my brother's wedding, she shocked the women as she sang one bawdy sang after another and danced away with abandon. The piece de resistance was her deadly dance of the seven veils to the accompaniment of a song that had her pleading:

I beg you, O fair Redcoat! Spare my blushes, I am married to a Brahmin!

Just before Lohaniji finally left, he gave me a lesson that I remembered for life. When I came to my mother's for the first time after getting married, I was miserable. I had never been taught to cook and sew and then was married into a family that was as conservative as ours was free. Lohaniji would often worry about my strange upbringing. He told my mother once, 'All she can do is read and ride a horse. Which Brahmin home do you imagine will value these arts?'

At home, we always had an army of helpers, so when I reached my father-in-law's home I was completely unprepared for the kind of work a daughter-in-law was expected to perform. Barbs were directed at my high educational degrees that had not equipped me for housework that even a child could handle.

I tried to hide my misery from my poor mother, who was grappling with so many problems then that this would have been the last straw. But I should have known that even with his failing eyesight, Lohaniji would spot my long face. 'How is it?' he asked and I burst into tears.

I sobbed out my miserable tale: how I was made to grind dal in a grinding stone, make complicated alpana patterns on the threshold, knead mountains of dough and then told to cook wearing just a sari and nothing else! All this while I listened to snide comments about my rich and spoilt childhood.

I waited for him to say, didn't I always warn you to learn some housekeeping? But for once he was silent. Then, he put a loving hand on my head and said, 'Don't cry, my child. Tell me, you have a good husband, don't you? The rest are just floating clouds, they will fly away. Have you ever seen what the Nepali coolies do when they carry huge loads on their backs? They first add a few stones to that load and walk up a hill, then when the worst is over, they shrug off the stones and race up. They never walk straight—always in a zig-zag, varying their pace. Have you seen that? Then learn from them, child. You will never need to weep again.'

~

As I recall my Almora days, two faces from my past seem to shake me and ask, 'Why haven't you written about us?' I can see them as they stand before me: the middle-aged Vaishnavi, her hand rattling a chimta (long iron tongs), and next to her, the emaciated Rajula, a begging bowl in her hand and a nose-ring shining on her pale face.

The first is the story of a nun, a Vaishnavi, who roamed from place to place—Badrinath, Kedarnath, Banaras, Haridwar, calling, *Alakh mai, bhiksha de!* In those days, you often came across such mendicants and I can recall several from my childhood, who wore long ropes of rudraksha round their necks and came to seek alms at our door in Almora. No householder ever turned them away. Perhaps people were more generous (read god-fearing) in my childhood. Every Saturday and Tuesday, two Nepali Vaishnavis came to our house, calling, *Alakh mai, bhiksha de!* Lohaniji would give them a large helping of rice and lentils in their bowl and they would leave but not before showering blessings on me, 'May you grow up to marry a prince, lalli. May you bring many brothers to this house—not one or two, but seven tall and strapping ones!'

Today would any house consider a crop of seven sons a blessing? No wonder I hear often harsh voices shoo away mendicants, 'Why can't you work? There is nothing wrong with you—get out! I don't give alms to idlers!' However, I still can't turn away such people when I meet them for my ears remember that sweet voice blessing me, 'May you grow up to marry a prince, lalli. May you bring many brothers to this house—not one or two, but seven tall and strapping ones!'

Then one day, a completely new and deep voice called out: *Alakh mai, bhiksha de!* I peeped out and saw a new Vaishnavi standing in the courtyard. Tall and strapping, with a small ochre bag slung on her shoulder, she was rattling a long pair of tongs in her hands. What arrested my attention was her size and appearance: she looked a man in drag! She stood there imperiously, looking around her for some human contact and finding none, called out, 'Alakh Niranjan! Mai will eat here today.' Interestingly, she used the masculine gender when talking of herself and I wondered if she were a woman at all. With her cropped hair she looked like a man, spoke like one and certainly had the voice of one. Her broad chest showed no sign of womanly breasts, and she was taller than any woman I had ever seen. Her flat nose had wide, flared nostrils that looked as if any minute now she would blow smoke out of them like a dragon!

She looked up and spotted me peering from behind a pillar on the veranda above the courtyard. 'You there, little girl,' she called to me. 'Did you hear me? Mai will eat here today, this is the Guru's wish. Go, tell someone inside.' Then she planted her tongs in a flower bed and settled down to wait.

I was terrified. We had long finished our morning meal; Lohaniji had locked up the kitchen and was probably asleep in his quarter. Where at this hour would I find food for this dragon?

'Mai, why don't you rest here?' I said politely. 'We have finished eating but let me ask my sister if she can get some bhiksha for you.'

'No!' she thundered and rattled her tongs noisily. 'Mai told you Mai shall eat here today. Go get Mai some firewood and pots and some besan, curds and chillies. Mai will eat karhi chawal today. Go!'

I was beginning to get a little irritated but there was an air of such authority about her that I found myself asking my sister to come and help me look for the ingredients for Mai's meal. By the time we reached the courtyard, Mai had once more planted her tongs close by and spread out her huge legs to make herself comfortable under our walnut tree.

'Come, children,' she greeted us, 'have you brought what Mai wants?' She leaned her bulk against the tree and squinted at us. We put down the lot before her and within minutes she had erected a makeshift stove with two stones, lit a fire and put a pot of karhi to cook. Then she began cleaning the rice and turned to us again.

'Alakh Guru! Do you want to ask anything? Mai does not come here often. She has come today because Guruji sent her.'

At first we couldn't understand what she meant; then she took a handful of rice grains and shut her eyes, mumbling some incomprehensible mantra. Both of us were thoroughly scared by now: who was this woman? A witch?

'What do you want to know? Something about the one you will marry?' she focussed her red eyes on us and they were glowing like coals.

'I have decided never to marry,' my sister said smugly. 'So I don't need to ask you anything about my future husband.' This was true: Jayanti had declared her decision quite firmly to our family a while ago and I think they had accepted it. But obviously, Mai knew something else. 'You will marry,' she told my sister firmly. 'No power on earth will ever stop that from happening.' She said this with such conviction that I could almost hear the sound of a band and a wedding procession outside our gates.

Then she broke the spell by turning her attention to her cooking and adopted a completely different tone as she started to chat with us. I watched her as she fiddled with the pots and pans: not only did she look like a man, she even had a faint

27

moustache on her upper lip. For a moment the same thought flashed through our heads: was this some wicked man who had come disguised as a woman to kidnap us? As if she could read our thoughts, Mai flashed her teeth at us, 'Scared you, did I?' and she suddenly grasped my hand. A shiver of pure horror ran through me: I felt as if a huge, slimy lizard had fallen on my hand. I still cannot describe what her touch was like without shuddering at the memory.

'Don't be put off by my face, child,' she said kindly. She sighed deeply as she ran a hand over her moustache, 'My name was Laxmi and when I came as a bride, my mother-in-law took one look at me and said to her son, "This is not a Laxmi, my son. This looks like a Laxman Singh." She and I became mortal enemies from that day on.' Her deep voice began to sound gruff now, as if she had a bad cold. Our eyes went to the beads around her neck and she introduced each one to us. 'This was given by the big Guru Maharaj when he accepted me as his disciple. This rosary, by the next Guru for saying my prayers and this one came from a cremation ground. These tulsi beads I picked up when I went for the Kumbh to Prayag.'

My sister got up and signalled to me to come inside as well but I was so enchanted by the stories the Vaishnavi had that I pretended I hadn't felt her nudge. The Vaishnavi did not see this side show as her attention was on her food. She first made three little morsels for her Gurus and turned to me, 'Want some?'

To tell you the truth, I was tempted at the sight of that spicy karhi but how could I possibly eat the alms I had given? I shook my head virtuously.

She finished her meal and scrubbed the pots and pans till they glistened, then picked a few embers from the dying fire to light her chillum. She foraged in her shoulder bag for a small red box and snorted some snuff into her huge nostrils. Then took a deep puff of her chillum and really became a dragon with smoke coming out of her nostrils.

'Vah,' she declared in a satisfied tone. 'Mai is very happy with you today, child.' I was fascinated at the size of her palm—and tried to imagine what a slap from her would mean. Was she a Vaishnavi or a wrestler?

'Do you really walk all day and night, Mai?' I asked

Her bloodshot eyes considered my question indulgently.

'Yes, child. Mai committed a terrible crime once. This is why God has cursed her to walk day and night, and never rest. She plants these tongs wherever her Guru commands her to and when she hears his voice she picks them up, says *Alakh*, and sets off again. Snowstorms, thunderstorms, raging torrents and streams—she has survived them all. She has sinned, child, so this is now her fate. She does whatever her Guru tells her to, whatever he tells her…'

She touched her hands reverently to her forehead at the mention of her Guru's name, then took a long puff from her chillum and floated off into a trance.

Guru? Where is he? What kind of Guru was this who she could hear yet I could not see? Was he a magician who whispered his command into her ears and then vanished?

'Ha, ha, ha!' the Vaishnavi roared with laughter. 'Silly child, how can *you* see Guru maharaj? He comes silently like a breeze and whispers in Mai's ears alone. He stays with Mai all the time, child. Day and night, wherever she goes, he goes with her and tells her not to be afraid—wherever she goes, whether the cremation ground, or the burning ghats.'

If she visited burning ghats and cremation grounds, how could she be a Vaishnavi, I wondered? Was she some tantric's disciple? The hair on my neck rose as I remembered something that had happened recently in our neighbourhood. A Vaishnavi came one day to their house, planted her tongs in their courtyard and established herself there. The simple housewife allowed her to stay on. There were rumours that the Vaishnavi offered meat and alcohol when she did her puja and brought terrible times to the host's family. First, they lost their newborn son, then the head of the family died and finally the lady of the house lost her mind. Then, as mysteriously as she had come, one day the Vaishnavi vanished. I began to tremble as I wondered whether this Vaishnavi was someone like that.

With her eyes still closed, my Vaishnavi began to speak in a low voice: 'Mai was ten years old when she got married and sent to her husband's home after four years. His name was Aan Singh and he ran a flourishing transport company. His lorries ran all over the terai—Tanakpur, Haldwani and Almora. Half the petrol went into the lorries, the other half into his belly. Used to come back drunk and then mother and son took turns to thrash Mai. Go fetch some wood, they would tell her. Or, go to the jungle and cut a bundle of grass for the cattle. Often, they sent her to graze the buffalo in the jungle. No one ever fed her a morsel or gave her even a sip of water. That bloody buffalo was another evil spirit—she would make poor Mai run all over the jungle and exhaust her. If Mai ever asked her mother-in-law, can I visit my mother, the witch would brand her with hot tongs for her cheeky request.'

At this point, Mai propped her chillum against the tree and rolled up her clothes: her torso was an ugly mass of weals, proof of the abuse she suffered in her husband's home. So she was a woman, I realized as I glanced furtively at her shrivelled breasts.

'One day, when Mai was burning with fever, her mother-in-law ordered her to take the buffalo for grazing to the jungle,' she went on with her story. 'Mai wept and pleaded, told her there was a leopard in the jungle too, and she said, "Good! If he eats you up, we'll get a proper daughter-in-law for this house."

'It seemed the wretched buffalo had been primed to torture Mai by the old hag—it was so frisky that day that Mai was run off her feet. Finally, the creature stood grazing at the edge of a ravine that rose in a sheer precipice from the raging waters of the Kali Ganga in the valley. If anyone toppled over not even a fragment of bone would survive. Mai was really angry that day, child, angry at her hunger, angry at the old hag, angry at her drunkard husband and decide to take it all out on that buffalo. She gave it one heave and down it plunged—sailing over the precipice like a blade of grass.

'Then Mai went home weeping and the old hag asked, What happened? Where is the buffalo, you wretch?

'In the jungle, saas-jyu. Come I'll show you, said Mai.

'Her cursing, screaming mother-in-law followed Mai to the jungle to the same ravine. The old woman was a thin, fragile creature and Mai a strapping young woman…

'Where is my precious buffalo, she screeched.

'There, said Mai, and pushed the old bag of bones over the edge. She went like a blade of grass, child, like a blade of grass…

'When Mai reached home, a furious Aan Singh was waiting for her with an axe in his hands. Drunk out of his mind, his eyes burning like coals.

'Where were you, whore, he yelled, how dare you come home alone? When you know a leopard roams that jungle, why did you take my mother there? Mai was livid: the bastard could think of his mother and his wretched buffalo, had he ever spared a thought for Mai?

'Your mother fell down a gorge, Mai wailed. Come quickly with me, she is hanging from a tree, we may be able to rescue her yet…

'Aan Singh ran to the spot. He swiped a blow across Mai's

31

cheek saying, What have you done to my mother? Where is she, you whore?

'There, said Mai, and shoved him down the sharp precipice to the raging Kali Ganga below. Mai never returned home after that, child, never. She went to a cave where a Nepali Guru maharaj lived, fell at his feet and confessed her crimes. Guru maharaj accepted her as his disciple and said, Go Mai, from now on roam the land and eat and wear what others give you. This is the penance you must perform for what you have done. From now on, remember, God alone will look after you, He is your only support...'

The Vaishnavi picked up her tongs and bag, dusted herself and stood up laughing. 'God bless you, child, Mai has to leave now...'

Before I could say anything or call my sister, she had descended the steps of the courtyard and vanished.

I used this masculine Vaishnavi as a character in two stories: 'Lati' and 'Dhuan'. Later, she made a sort of guest appearance in my novel *Chaudah Phere*. Her extraordinary story continues to haunt me till today. In one day, this woman had snuffed not one but three lives—a buffalo, a mother-in-law and a husband. And yet can anyone deny that she did not have a reason? No court heard of this triple murder, no lawmaker pronounced a judgement on her and no jailor kept her in prison. She became her own jailor and the chains on her feet were clamped there by her own conscience. But what fascinated me the most was the fourth murder she committed but never spoke of: when she stood at the edge of the precipice and decided to hurl her youth, her dreams and desires forever into the raging torrents of the Kali Ganga. They floated down that ravine like a blade of grass and left a celibate Vaishnavi where a young girl once stood.

Did any law court ever pronounce a more terrible punishment?

And now, another prisoner of conscience stands before my eyes.

I first met Rajula under the same walnut tree where the Vaishnavi had planted her tongs. Rajula carried a small tambourine in her hand and sang the Riturain songs of spring in a high, sweet voice. In the Almora of my childhood, bands of professional folk singers would arrive in March at the start of spring, and go from one prominent home to another to entertain them with the traditional folk songs of the season at *Chaitra baithaks*, or private spring concerts. Unlike professional singing girls, there was no trace of the bazaar about these women. They wore velvet ghagras trimmed with lace and their faces were discreetly veiled with odhnis. Their tinkling laughter rang through dull courtyards and lit up the lives of these stern Brahmin havelis.

Another, rather less attractive, tradition of those days also comes to my mind. Several older men from the high-born Brahmin families in Kumaon had installed a singing girl as a mistress in their homes. A 'Ram' was prefixed to the name of the singing girl to make it 'kosher' so that it was possible to meet a Ramkatori, Rampriya or Rampyari at an uncle's house. Naturally, the most lively *Chaitra baithaks* were organized in homes where one of their own lived as the mistress of the householder. Unfortunately, no one in our neighbourhood had such a patroness but that did not stop us from running to the window whenever we heard a band of them go singing their way to a *baithak*.

One day, I went across to a granduncle's house to borrow their newspaper. I barged into his private sitting area and will never forget what I saw. My granduncle, cigar in hand, was reclining on a bolster surrounded by giggling apsaras. My eyes were dazzled by the colours of their bright clothes and the scent

33

of their bodies. It seemed as if someone had sprinkled a dozen bottles of perfume in the room. For a moment, the old man was nonplussed at the sight of his grandniece but recovered his composure quickly. With remarkable aplomb, considering his posture and surroundings, he asked me kindly, 'What brings you here, child?'

'I wanted to borrow the *Statesman*,' I stammered.

'Oh, is this your granddaughter, Lalla? We must sing the first song of Chaitra for her, in that case,' one apsara smiled. And before my granduncle or I could say anything, I was surrounded, like a queen bee by her worker bees, by their honey-sweet voices:

May this auspicious day
Come a thousand times
In the lives of our daughters…

I was touched, caressed and smothered with those hands and voices. Unused to such loving touches on my body, I was nearly reduced to tears with embarrassment. Sensing my discomfiture, my granduncle said sharply, 'What is all this? Go child,' he said gently to me, 'the paper is lying there. Pick it up and take it home.'

The old man was a widower and childless to boot. Perhaps his mistress, longing for a child to fuss over, was responsible for that episode. Years later, Maupassant's 'Madame Tellier's Establishment' reminded me strongly of that day. Maupassant's story is about the madame who runs an eponymous brothel, Madame Tellier's, and who takes her lively, giggling band of prostitutes to attend a niece's baptism. He describes brilliantly the havoc that ensues in the Catholic home of her brother as this exotic band of Parisian butterflies descends on a simple village.

My ears still ring with the sweet Riturain song, set to Raga Desh, that they sang for me that day.

May this auspicious day
Come a thousand times
In the lives of our daughters…

So when Rajula came with her tambourine to our courtyard singing the same song, I was stunned. She was dark and her eyes were deep pools of sadness. Her sweet voice had an attractive break and rose with a nasal twang, like the plaintive wail of a shehnai. I now realize that she was probably syphilitic for her nose had collapsed and that is probably why her voice had that unique timbre.

'What shall I sing for you, lalli?' she asked me. 'Riturain, Pari Chanchari or Ramola…?'

She came almost every day and her fund of folksongs had all of us eating out of her hands. She generously shared her treasure trove with me and I eagerly learnt as many as I could to take back to Santiniketan. Kanika Devi, Jyotishdev Burman and Suchitra Mitra were my contemporaries and we often used these lovely Pahari tunes in our impromptu concerts. Tilak Kamod, Desh and Durga—these were the three ragas that gave life to the folksongs of Kumaon. Rajula had learnt them from her mother and given them a flavour all her own. She was born to sing and when I hear the Malwa folksongs of Kumar Gandharva, I remember her artless and unselfconscious singing with new respect. She took a note to the highest pitch and left it there to float in silence—then after a pause she would pick it up from the base and play with it as if it were a kite.

She had no accompaniments, just a small battered tambourine. Often she lit a flame to warm its sagging skin and bring it to

35

life. Then, she would shut her eyes, place a hand on her ear and sing. When she sang *Beru pako bara masa*... that famous Kumaoni folksong that everyone has heard, I swear even the walnuts on our tree turned red with passion.

'Rajula, where did you learn to sing like this?' I asked her once.

'From Him,' she closed her eyes and pointed heavenwards.

No human being could have given her that voice, so Rajula was right: her voice had to be a divine gift. She sang all the Riturain songs—Bhagnaula, Ramola, the lot—but when she sang a hymn called *Kariye chhima*, she was scintillating.

What I have said, or left unsaid
What I heard, or did not hear
What I did, or left undone
Forgive me for all that, my Lord!

She would go into a trance, her eyes streaming with tears as she asked Him for forgiveness. I have seen her move her audience to tears when she sang her special song.

'Why do you have to beg when you have such a voice, Rajula?' I asked once. By now, she and I had a special bond that grew from our shared love for music. Rajula became silent.

'Don't ask, lalli. By the grace of people such as yourself, Rajula earned so much that she could have built ten such palaces for herself by now,' she replied, pointing to our haveli. For a moment, something like pride lit up the pools of darkness in her eyes.

'So,' I prompted her, 'where did all that money go?'

'Into the river,' she said as she dropped the tambourine into her lap.

'Don't joke, Rajula.' I held her hands as I begged her.' Tell me where that money went.'

'What is the use of that, lalli?' she asked sadly. 'You come from a high-born Brahmin home, lalli, your touch can wash away the sins of a fallen woman like me. But you are my Gangajal, my holy water, lalli, I cannot hold your hand and lie. I threw away forty tolas of gold…'

'Forty tolas of gold?' I gasped.

'Yes, lalli,' she nodded tonelessly.

'Not just that,' she went on. 'Four thousand silver coins with "Vittoria's" face on them, I threw those into the Bhagirathi as well.'

'But why did you do such an insane thing, Rajula? You have to beg for your food now, why, when you had so much, did you…?'

'There was a reason, lalli, I had sinned. Committed a heinous crime. I was just not caught, that's all. God must have shut His eyes that day,' she said and gave a wan smile. Then her pale face went paler and she muttered, 'I killed someone, lalli.'

I held my breath.

'I killed my own son.'

I peered into her face but her eyes were dry; perhaps she had used up all her tears.

'Why,' I whispered, 'why did you do such a thing, Rajula?'

'Because he was the spitting image of his father, lalli. When I could see his father's features on his face from the minute he was born, just imagine what would happen when he grew up and went out in the world? Everyone would know whose child he was.' She took a deep breath and went on in a steady voice, 'So I took him to the river, shut my eyes and held him there until he drowned.'

What a strange woman this was! Most mothers would consider it a badge of pride to give birth to a son who resembled his father and here was Rajula who had killed hers for this reason.

'You won't understand, lalli,' she answered my unspoken question as she patted me kindly. 'My whole village used to worship his father and, after all, I was not even his wedded wife. I was a lowly singing girl, God's handmaiden, the fallen scarlet woman of the village. How could I let his name be tarnished? I ran away from the village that night and dropped all my worldly goods in the Bhagirathi. Don't ask me what I suffered and where I went after that, lalli. May God forgive us all!' She touched her hands reverently to her forehead.

'God punished me for that crime: I lost my voice, dreadful sores broke out all over my body, lalli. I was like a leper who people shunned and moved away from. Occasionally a kind soul would toss a few coins my way as I lay under a tree. And the nightmares!' She shuddered as she recalled them. 'I dreamt my clothes were drenched with the milk from my breasts, I wanted to scream but no sound came from my throat any more. Then one day, I sang *Kariye chhima*, the song you love. And a miracle took place. My voice came back! The voice I had lost. Now I walk from home to home and sing *Kariye chhima*, lalli. This is the penance God has decided I must perform and I bow to His will.'

Rajula must have died singing that song by now but her tambourine and the tinkle of her voice come back ever so often to me. Years later, Rajula became the heroine of my novella *Kariye Chhima*, and I felt as if I had finally been able to repay the woman who taught me more beautiful music than I ever heard.

Rajula and the Vaishnavi opened my eyes to a truth that I have grappled with ever since. That there is no jail on earth that can shackle a free spirit and no spirit so free that its feet cannot be bound in chains we cannot see.

2

Ama

Diddi's vivid childhood memories are as deeply frustrating as they are compelling. The wall she erected around her inner life and fears is impenetrable and guards a kingdom where she will grant entry very reluctantly, if at all.

In contrast to her evocative pictures of Lohaniji, Henry Pant, Alakh Mai and Rajula is Diddi's stubborn refusal to confront the dark history of her own family, or indeed her own life. Her sharp eyes saw the shadows, yet she resolutely refused to expose the people she loved the most to ridicule or criticism. I think she sincerely hoped she could transform the nature of her past with the power of selective recall and that if she did not remember the unhappiness and doubts of her past, they would simply disappear. So she blotted out the sun by holding up a thumb. How right Edna St Vincent Millay was when she declared that 'Childhood is a kingdom where…mothers and fathers don't die.'

In her portrait of Lohaniji, Diddi refers to the sudden death of her father in faraway Bangalore so lightly that it is almost invisible. Her tone does not vary dramatically, nor does the confident voice wobble, as she goes over the time when the proud Kasoon Pandes were reduced to penury. She relates almost matter-of-factly how Ama returned to Almora, a widow at forty with nine children to look after and Kasoon lost its golden sheen. 'Gaps and holes appeared everywhere as one valuable heirloom after another was sold off,' she says, and that is all we hear. Significantly, the episode comes in the middle, not the end, of her childhood reminiscences. It was a hint that the resilient spirit of the family refused to be defeated by this tragic turn and yet it troubled me that there was nothing about the indomitable spirit of the Kasoon women until I came to Diddi's portrait of her mother: Ama to us grandchildren.

Diddi begins her last book, *Sone De*, with a moving portrait of her mother, a lengthy and loving homage to the strong matriarch who had a profound influence on the lives of all her children. Highly readable and replete with the anecdotes that Diddi knits so deftly into her portraits it is, nevertheless, deafeningly silent on some crucial histories. I have, therefore, included an essay my sister Mrinal wrote on Ama in 1981, soon after Ama's death, in a journal called *Mainstream*, to offset the idyllic picture that Diddi paints of her childhood. Mrinal presents a picture free of the romantic clutter that clouded Diddi's vision and is closer to the spirit of the Ama I remember. She looks at Ama straight in the eye and uncovers her not merely as a heroic, if eccentric, character but as the defining symbol of the Kasoon clan: its Mother Courage.

I strongly believe that all daughters ultimately grow up to be like their mothers and as Diddi grew older, she became another Ama. Outspoken and frank, often brutally and undiplomatically so, she spared no one, herself included. Ama's most admirable quality had always been her refusal to accept injustice or hypocrisy quietly: a quality she generously passed on to Diddi. This is why they both were such lonely characters in their last years although they remained remarkably free of bitterness and retained their sense of humour to the end. It is perhaps no curious coincidence that Diddi's life was such a close mirror of her mother's for if character is destiny, then Diddi's later life—like Ama's—was predetermined by her own nature. Ama was widowed at forty, Diddi at fifty. Both struggled hard to survive the loss of money, home and support. Yet they both survived and—even though they were such champions of male supremacy—both chose to come to their daughters when it was time to die.

Obviously, clan histories—like histories of nations—repeat themselves endlessly.

When we were growing up, Ama to us was a figure larger than life. Her house dominated every aspect of our childhood and each one of us twenty-odd grandchildren remember her as an intimidating, often despotic, matriarch who laid the law in Kasoon and was both feared and admired across the town. For a person who broke tradition and gave as good as she got to the snotty Kumaoni Brahmin community, Ama was also responsible for breeding in all those she brought up a respect for tradition and patriarchal laws. She was unashamedly partial to the boys of the family and gave them a latitude that her granddaughters were never allowed. Laughing loudly, whistling and talking out of turn were some no-nos for us girls. However, she was also proud of what her girls achieved and the first to write to us when any of us girls did well. Ama always referred to husbands as 'malik' (owner) for that is how she perceived the man-woman relationship in an ideal marriage. So she ordered the universe around her in the image of a morality that she believed had stood the test of time. Any subversion of the traditional domestic hierarchy earned her severe displeasure. Thus, although she was inordinately proud of Diddi, she was equally afraid that her success as a writer would make her more important than her husband and that would never do. Diddi's need for a strong male presence and a defined boundary within which to operate, I am reasonably sure, had its roots in the laws her mother had taught her to trust.

This curious dichotomy would create a lifelong tussle in Diddi's life as she struggled to reconcile her naturally liberal personality with the strict patriarchal morality of her mother's Brahmanical world. Diddi disapproved loudly of what she saw as threats to a 'moral' way of living—marriages outside the community, divorces, live-in relationships, back-chatting elders, questioning unfair traditions. Yet, paradoxically, she wrote novels and stories that had strong women characters who rebelled against all such values and social inequalities. This also accounted for her lifelong fascination with those who lived on the margins—mendicants, lunatics and lepers. Time and again, she returns in her short stories and novels to characters drawn from those to whom rigid social values cannot be applied.

She took an unreasonable dislike to a friend of mine who had divorced her husband and was living with a married man. Things were so bad that whenever this friend came to visit me, Diddi would not come to the dining table. 'What childishness is this?' I asked her. 'If I had done what my friend has, I could perhaps have understood your behaviour. But this is absurd—how can you be so insulting to a guest?'

'You know what I feel about women who break up homes and marriages,' she replied sulkily.

'Then what about your friend S in Lucknow?' I asked, naming a close friend of hers who had created a stir when she married a famous surgeon of the town, forced him to abandon his first wife and family and move in with her.

Diddi flounced out of the room. Logic and reasonableness

were unknown commodities in Ama's daughters. And although they laid the law, they seldom followed it.

~

Ama

Diddi writes:

The delightful aroma of fragrant tobacco came out to embrace us lovingly as soon as we reached my Nana's house in Lucknow. Inside, in Nana's sitting room, my mother's brother (whom we called Mama) sat playing bridge with his friends, a hukka in one hand and cards in the other. Mama's bridge buddies—among them the famous lawyer Sir Tej Bahadur Sapru and Rajrajeshwar Bali—were sprawled comfortably against the bolsters and sparkling white sheets spread over the carpets. Drinks were being served and delicious snacks, such as tender green peas cooked with spices, sent up from the kitchen. It seemed to us children, fresh from Almora and another grandfather's house, as if everyone in this grandfather's house always laughed and had fun. Never have I heard such happy laughter again—the open and pure sound of it still makes me smile.

Mama went to the university in the morning in his buggy that would arrive on the dot of nine to wait for him in the porch. As soon as we heard the tinkle of the bells and wheels, we'd race down and dance round the horse, chafing and stamping his feet impatiently. Mama's bridge game had still not ended and paans were now being served in the sitting room. Garlands of them strung from silver chains emerged from the huge paandaan that my Nani presided over. We could hear her grumbling, cursing the bridge players as she sent in tray upon tray of food and paans to Mama's guests.

Someone would come and announce that we were being called inside for breakfast, which was invariably hot jalebis from a shop near the pir's grave. These were fat, juicy sweets we washed down with glasses of hot milk topped with thick swirls of cream. Mama would finally deign to go to the university, and amble towards the porch. The coachman leapt to his seat and his valet, Mahabali, would take his position behind him. The tall and menacing Mahabali wore an amulet round his neck to ward off the evil eye and we wondered who would dare to cast it on his fearful face.

The buggy set off in a tinkle of bells and, with Mama's departure, the rhythms of the house changed dramatically. A new stream of visitors now entered the house via the courtyard: the first to arrive was the naoon (the barber's wife), to give the women an oil massage and bathe the children. She went from house to house carrying gossip and with each drop of oil she rubbed in a fresh scandal about the families in the area. Next came the bangle-seller, who arrived every fortnight to change our bangles. How she coaxed those dainty glass bangles over our wrists without breaking them was a mystery to me. 'Nani, please,' we pleaded, 'can we wear different ones this time?' According to Nani, if young girls did not wear bangles, their wrists became hard and tough like a man's. Since they had a functional, rather than a decorative, purpose another set of plain bangles replaced the old ones. 'No, you will wear what I want you to wear!' was the verdict. Nani hated having her decisions crossed and her face would flush ominously. Even when she was past seventy, my grandmother, with her Grecian nose, rosy face and delicate eyebrows, was beautiful. Her hair always smelt of the fragrant jasmine oil that came specially for her from Asghar

Ali's and her regal bearing remained unchanged till the end.

The women would now sit in the courtyard to cut vegetables and clean the rice and dals. As visiting granddaughters, Jayanti and I were given lighter duties. Her old maid, Ramdeyi, would tease Nani, 'Bahuji, don't spoil these girls too much! Sons you can wear like tilak on your forehead, but girls must be taught how to stoke the fires in the kitchen.' Ramdeyi, a childless widow, had moved into my grandfather's house to work in the kitchen after she retired from her job at Balrampur Hospital.

My grandfather was the leading doctor of Lucknow and laid the foundation of the city's landmark Balrampur Hospital. He was the family physician to the Raja of Balrampur and had persuaded him to donate some land for a charitable hospital. Nana also persuaded another rich patient, Lala Puttulal, to open a purdah school for girls: Puttulal donated a house for this and this is how Lucknow's famous Mahila College was started off. Among its first five students was my mother; she had a photo album she won as a prize with an inscription from Harcourt Butler, the British Resident of Oudh: 'Presented to Leelawati Pant for standing first in the eighth class.'

I also remember a huge oil painting of my grandfather and a bust made by a grateful patient that used to hang in the sitting room. Pandit Motilal Nehru came once and all of us peeped from behind curtains to catch a glimpse of him. On another occasion, Raja Saheb Manda (whose son, Viswanath Pratap Singh, later became a prime minister) took off his Karakul cap and placed it on a table nearby. My cousin Krishna, always up to mischief, ran away with it. The uproar that took place as servants chased Krishna all over the house to get the cap back is another memory.

But let us return to my Nani's courtyard where lunch is over. It is the turn of the hawkers and vendors to walk through the lanes behind the house and tempt us. On the dot of one, I swear you could set your watch by this, we heard the voice of a man who sold sugared fruits. For two paise a piece, you could take your pick: mangoes from Malihabad, grapes, jamuns, louquats and ripe speckled bananas. Next came the ice-candy man, with bottles of lurid colours to sprinkle over chips of ice shaved into a terracotta cup. One anna was his price. Then came the vendor of combs, mirrors, paste jewellery, ribbons and kohl. Occasionally, a Bengali sari-seller would call, *Kapod!* And we'd race down to see what saris he had in his bundle. At the sight of his lace-trimmed petticoats (straight from Calcutta, Didi, he claimed) our hearts swung like a pendulum as he held its swaying folds in front of us. A little later a Gujarati couple came with their bioscope. For two paise we saw a dhobin who weighed nine maunds, Mecca and Medina and a lover pulling a thorn from his mistress's foot. No matter how often we heard the old man's sing-song commentary, we never tired of the magical, moving pictures.

The only pleasure banned to us was a visit to a nautanki. And there was a reason. Apparently, a simple Pahari servant from my Nana's staff once went there and lost his heart to the leading lady, fell hopelessly in love with her and committed suicide. Once, only after days of cajoling, my grandmother allowed us to go and see a show with Mahabali the Fearful as our escort.

Occasionally, Mama would take us to Aminabad to eat chaat at a famous shop that stood near the Begum Hazrat Mahal Park. Run by an old man who wore the typical dupaliya topi of those times and a starched white chikan kurta, the shop opened only at five in the evening and people thronged to eat the golgappas and hari matar ki chaat he served. To wash it down, he sold an ambrosial drink made of iced aniseed balls. It was said that this drink was the best guard against exposure to the dreaded loo winds.

~

Years later, when my mother lay dying, she asked me once,

'Will you take me one day to Babu's kothi?'

I knew that the old house was a ruin now and a shanty town had sprung up on its sprawling grounds. It had passed through many hands and all that remained of the old days was a pair of marble lions on the gates. They say my grandfather's name (Dr Hardutt Pant) can still be read on the marble nameplate studded into the gates.

We both knew that my mother's request was a like a child asking to be taken to the moon. She could neither move nor see. What will you do if I take you there, I asked her indulgently.

She looked at me with such longing in her eyes that I caught my breath.

'I'll shout: Amma! I've come back to you!' she replied.

~

A photograph of my mother, we called her Ija, taken just after she was married used to hang in her father's house and later in Kasoon. It is imprinted in my mind so clearly that I can still see her solemn face gazing at the camera. Her tiny frame is almost smothered in a heavy silk sari with a rich gold border and every bit of her is dripping with ornaments—ropes of pearls round her neck, long earrings, bangles and rings.

We never actually saw these historic jewels except in that photograph for by the time we grew up, Ija had given away every one of them or used them to buy whatever was needed to bring up the family after she was widowed. 'This necklace,' she pointed out a heavy diamond-studded piece in the picture to us gawping children, 'was given by the Nawab of Daulatpur when I got married, these bangles by the Raja of Gauba...'

'But where are they now?' we asked.

'That one I sold to marry off Nan Gusain and build his house, these bangles I hawked when I married Panchi Bai…' she listed the lost treasures without a trace of regret. Like the Statue of Liberty, Ija turned our house into a shelter for the homeless and destitute. Among the many people my mother collected around her was a beautiful child widow called Mohini, who was about my brother Tribhi's age. Mohini, called Munna by all of us, was sent back by her husband's family after his death so that she could be looked after by her brothers. Munna's brothers were friends of my father's only brother, a bachelor all his life who later became a hermit. The older one, a handsome rake called Chani Mastan (Merry Chani) went hunting one day and never returned. They found his body three days later in the jungles behind Cheena Peak in Nainital. Her second brother, called Dajyu by everyone for his generous nature, was a university teacher. After he died of tuberculosis, my uncle took Munna to Ma Anandmayi's ashram for how could he, a bachelor, look after a young and beautiful girl? When Ija heard this, she went flying across to the ashram to rescue her. Munna was scheduled to take her vows as a nun the next day, and they were preparing to shave off her hair. Ija's heart melted at the sight of this beautiful girl, sitting quietly with her head resting on her knees, and she decided then and there to take Munna back with her and bring her up as her own child.

'How can a girl of her age be forced to forsake the world?' she asked my uncle angrily. 'Munna will stay here and become my tenth child. She will go to Santiniketan with Jayanti and Gaura and that is that.' So Munna came with us when we went back to Santiniketan that year and became a disciple of Nandlal Bose in Kala Bhavan. Before she left Almora, my mother slipped glass bangles on her wrists, threw out her white widow's weeds and gave her a stack of bright saris to wear. Ija then put a bindi on Munna's forehead and told her, 'Remember Munna, if you have a clear conscience then there is no need to fear anyone. Forget what the world will say—why care for people who will talk anyway?'

No one can understand now how radical and subversive this decision was in Almora in those days. For years, a whispering campaign was launched by spiteful people against Ija. People even said that she was grooming Munna to join the Nawab of Rampur's harem as my father was the Home Minister there. Ija stood her ground: she dared anyone to come and say this to her face. No one did.

~

In one of her last letters to me Ija wrote: 'I have seen more deaths than I care to remember and God knows how many more I am destined to see... The biggest curse of old age is that people hide things from you, assuming that they will not be able to deal with bad news. What rubbish this is! Old age can dim all your senses but your sixth sense becomes more acute as you grow older. I can hardly see any more, my hearing is not what it was but my personal warning system alerts me about which of my children is in trouble.

'How are you? What exactly is wrong with you? One last order from me to all of you: none of you are allowed to leave this world before me. I have taken so many knocks that I do not know whether I care to take another...'

~

What knocks she had weathered! The death of my sister Chanda and her husband, who left two small infants in her care. Then

49

my father went, a few years later his brother too and with them the days of happiness and plenty. It was as if a macabre game of snakes and ladders had cursed her to come down to 2 after having reached 99. Perhaps it was this that made her treat life as a joke to be laughed away. Till her death, she kept us amused with her antics and her sharp tongue spared no one. One incident brings out her spirit of resilience most vividly to me.

A few years ago, kerosene oil went underground in Almora and the grocer who had opened a shop just outside Kasoon promised to send her some. Ija sent him four empty bottles for refilling. And waited. Then she was told that the wretch had sent the whole consignment to some officer in the town. She sent her servant to ask him what had happened to the promised bottles of kerosene. He was sorry there was just enough to fill one bottle, he replied, and the servant flashed the solitary bottle in front of Ija's furious face. 'Wait,' she told her servant. She hobbled across to her secret hoard, pulled out two bottles she had stashed away and added a box of matches and wrote a note to the grocer. It read:

'You wretched worm, I am sending you some bottles of kerosene and a box of matches. Pour the oil on you head and set it aflame with my matches. Today is Baikunth Ekadasi, I promise you will go straight to heaven.'

~

Ama

My sister Mrinal writes:

'...When arthritis and failing eyesight had practically confined Ama to her chair and forced her to come and live with my mother—the daughter she fought with, scolded and loved the most, I spent a long lazy month with her in my mother's house in Lucknow. As she reminisced about her past, I began to see an Ama I had never known, and in whose life-story I saw the tragedy of a whole generation that was great and sick at the same time, and the beastly double standards that romanticized this frail little woman, yet made near-impossible demands on her.

Ama was married to my grandfather at the age of seven, when her husband was eighteen. Her first child, a daughter, was born when she was fourteen. This daughter was also married at the age of twelve and gave birth to a son next year, so Ama became an Ama at the age of twenty-seven. The youngest child of an eminent doctor from Lucknow, Ama had grown up in the cultured and liberal—if somewhat decadent—ethos of a feudal Lucknow. She recalled many all-night concerts of classical music and dance when she sat with her parents and saw stalwarts like Kalka-Bindadin perform. Ama spoke no Kumaoni till she got married. Her in-laws, the long-nosed Pandes of Kasoon, were aristocratic, aloof and extremely conservative and spoke only Kumaoni at home. Her father-in-law was an eminent Sanskrit scholar and a terror in the town of Almora. In the early twenties, when Ama was a young bride, he was spearheading a local campaign against the Brahmin who had chosen to go to Japan for 'further studies' and returned with a degree in medicine. This young doctor demanded he be rehabilitated after the routine prayaschit (expiation) performed by the licking of the panchgavya (a mixture of five purifying elements including the dung and urine of a cow). The Kasoon stand was that if this young impudent Anglophile was taken back into the fold, not only would the purest of the pure Kumaoni Brahmins be polluted, it would also encourage all like-minded young aspirants to go abroad and eat cow-flesh, and then come back and demand to take panchgavya and be purified again. No! he thundered, once a mlechcha (outcaste) by association, always a mlechcha!

The liberals among the Kumaoni Brahmins, one of them Ama's doctor father, were in favour of elasticizing the rigid boundaries of Brahminism. He felt that if they continued to be rigid, they would lose most of their intelligent young men. (One of the chief reasons for the doctor's stand was that his own son was by then studying law in England.) Enraged by the betrayal of his own kinsman, Ama's father-in-law ruled that thenceforth she was not to step into her father's house. If she did, he'd get his son another wife. So the battle-lines were firmly drawn. The conservatives, headed by the Kasoon clan, were grouped on one side and the liberals, headed by the doctor and his relatives of the local Champa Naula clan, were on the other. All interaction between the two groups ceased. When Ama's only brother, the England-returned barrister, got married, she was not permitted to attend the wedding, but made to put on her heaviest jewellery and her finest clothes and shower flowers on the wedding procession from the rooftop as the wedding party passed the road below Kasoon.

Ama, in her own words, was like a calf torn from its mother's udders. Her mother too wept day and night, till one summer her irate husband bought her another house in Almora where she could see her beloved child from the rooftop. That summer the ingenious mother and daughter, helped by numerous sympathetic aunts and great-aunts of the town, developed a modus operandi whereby the family sweeper, in exchange for a handsome sum of money, would escort the young bride through the back door of the toilet of her father's house, where the mother joined her with generous gifts of clothes and sweets and family gossip for a few minutes before Ama was escorted back again.

Like all supposedly foolproof plans, this too didn't work for too long. One day, as she returned, Ama found her father-in-law coughing and walking to and fro near the back entrance. 'Where were you?' he thundered and Ama froze. He then declared that she was dead for the Kasoon Pandes now and could go back to the toilet she'd come from. By this time, an enormous courtyard was filled with curious and interested onlookers, who tut-tutted for the poor daughter-in-law but dared not defy the angry old man. 'After much ramlila,' to quote Ama, it was resolved that a mock shraddha—a ghatashraddha—be performed and Ama be rechristened and remarried to her husband. This was duly done. A clay pitcher with holy water—symbolizing Ama's body—was destroyed and Ama was considered reborn. 'That was the day,' Ama said, 'I ceased to worry about an afterlife or being alone.'

Soon after this, Ama lost her mother-in-law and her husband lost his faith in tradition. He confided to his young wife that he had begun eating meat, and that he too had bought a passage to England. However, she was to keep this secret until he returned from England after two years. So Ama, dying inwardly of worry, lied smoothly to her father-in-law and told him that his son had gone down south to study. Since women were supposed to be vague about most affairs of the world outside, the lie was accepted. Soon, however, an anonymous letter arrived asking the old man sarcastically: 'How does it feel now that your own son has gone to the land of the mlechchas, huh? Do you still feel the same way about ostracizing the foreign-returned young man?'

Like Bhishma Pitamah, her father-in-law, Ama said, made a terrible vow: that he would go to Kashi and die on the banks of the Ganga like a sanyasi, in expiation of his son's ultimate sin. He was almost blind in both eyes by now, but he left. Ama was left all alone with her nine children, in a town that in those days did not permit unescorted Brahmin women out on the streets or in the market. Kumaon in those days was an island barely connected with the railhead in the faraway town of Bareilly by a dangerous road, difficult to traverse even for a physically fit male. Yet Ama refused to dissolve into tears. Instead, she gathered her brood, called for her loyal servants, and left by palki, holding in her lap her youngest child and a paandaan with her jewellery. The rest of her children followed with the servants. Somehow this circus managed to reach Banaras, locate and placate the irate and dejected patriarch, and bring him back. 'Men's presence you need next to you always,' she told me, 'even if they are only man-shaped lumps of dough. No one likes to see a woman managing things, see?'

… Ama was to face greater travails later. She became a widow before she was forty, saw her nineteen-year-old son TK return from Santiniketan and step into his father's job in the state of Orchcha, then opt for the Indian Police Service and…die young like his father. After this, for most of her remaining years, Ama remained in the ancestral home that went to pieces around her, with poverty, with neglect. Yet no one, not even her own children, mourned the wasted life of this spirited woman, or blamed the socio-political changes for the decline in her life as they did in the case of my uncle. Men had let her down again and again, yet to the women of Ama's generation, men were the only weapons—even if they cut both ways—women had. And she was determined that men, who are ultimately in control of women's lives, even if they cannot control their own, must be controlled—if necessary by guile. The lack of this last quality in my mother was always a source of worry to her.

… She often told us that after her husband died suddenly of a carbuncle in Bangalore, there was no one she could turn to.

So she had to bring the body home from the mortuary, arrange for the funeral all by herself, and then sell off the huge house and all the furnishings to buy the passage back to Almora for herself, her children and her servants. 'In that one week my tears went back into my head and my hair turned completely white,' she used to say. I think she told us that story again and again to purge herself of the horror of a whole week when she was left alone without men, without moorings. This was what turned her into the woman I remember: a lonely, somewhat cantankerous figure, who constantly offended the community and her daughters-in-law with her blunt pronouncements about social mores, but who had an unerring nose for sniffing out hypocrisy.

3

Santiniketan

In 1902, the poet Tagore created a new academy of learning in the deep recesses of the tribal Santhal belt near Bolpur in West Bengal and called it Santiniketan, the Abode of Peace. Although he belonged to one of the most prominent feudal families of Bengal, Tagore displayed little interest in the life of leisure and idle pursuits that others of his birth revelled in. In fact, he held its lifestyle responsible for creating unbridgeable rifts between parents and children and has written evocatively of the remote relationship he had with his own parents. By the time Tagore created Santiniketan, he had lost his own children—both his daughters to tuberculosis and his only son to cholera. He was already a famous man, India's first Nobel laureate and hailed as a quintessential Renaissance figure of those times, so in material terms there was nothing more that he sought from the Calcutta crowd. The creation of Santiniketan was for him, in a sense, a retreat into a life of contemplation far away from the mannered life of the Bengal aristocracy.

More than a radical educational experiment, Santiniketan was a defiant nationalist gesture against the Macaulayan educational system the British had introduced to create babus and clerks for their government. A great wave of patriotic resurgence was sweeping across India under the inspiring call of Mahatma Gandhi, and Tagore was one of several Indian thinkers and prominent educationists who wished to make pedagogy an instrument of change. Diddi's own grandfather was one of the founders of the Banaras Hindu Viswavidyalaya, a university to provide to Indian students an Indian education that had its roots in the ancient oral tradition and where teachers and students shared a relationship based on that of a family. Yet, strangely enough, it was not to Banaras but to distant Santiniketan that he decided to send his own grandchildren. The reason is not far to see.

Among the pictures I inherited from Diddi's collection is a framed photograph of her father, called Hubby by everyone. It shows him, a handsome young man in his thirties, sitting on a chair in a studio, cigar in hand, dressed in a morning coat and cravat. On his head is a dashing turban that all officials of princely courts wore in those days and he exudes an unmistakable aura of elegance and confidence. He also looks remarkably like Diddi.

Hubby was the antithesis of his father: he smoked and drank, lived a westernized life and was more at home in the club than in his father's austere Brahmin world. Among his friends were princes and rulers, thinkers, writers and poets. He was a regular contributor to the *Asia Magazine* and the library in Kasoon had several books on English poetry and essays with his flamboyant signature on the flyleaf. One of these was an autographed copy of Jim Corbett's *Man-eaters of Kumaon*, signed 'To my affectionate friend Ashwini, Jim Corbett'. Hubby's father could not understand these Anglophile leanings and was alarmed at the prospect of his grandchildren turning into brown sahibs. This is why my uncle Tribhi was drawn away from Miss Mumford's clutches and the three eldest children were kept under the eagle eye of Lohaniji in Almora. When it was time

57

for them to go to regular school, their grandfather chose to send them so far away that their own father would never poison their lives with the hedonistic lifestyle of the princely states. In fact, Diddi's grandfather looks remarkably like Tagore—he wore the same long habit and had a long, flowing beard, and hair.

In those days, there was no motor road between Almora and Kathgodam, the nearest railhead. Diddi and her siblings walked the 25-odd miles to reach it, chaperoned by Lohaniji and two old servants. The caravan consisted of some Nepali coolies who carried their luggage and the journey was accomplished in two stages. Lohaniji supervised the food for the children when they set camp but they preferred to sneak across to the tantalizing 'fish curry' that the Nepali coolies cooked. Diddi told us how the coolies were so poor that they picked smooth pebbles from the stream near their camp and dropped them in the broth of onions and water to flavour them with a 'fish' taste. Both she and my uncle Tribhi—lifelong epicures and devoted carnivores— dodged the eagle-eyed Lohaniji and Jayanti to beg the coolies for a portion of their dinner.

Diddi loved her years at Santiniketan and imbibed all she could from its free and open teaching system. She quickly learnt to speak Bengali and, in fact, her first short story was written not in Hindi but in Bengali. I have a theory that those who have a good musical ear also have a natural facility for learning languages and am convinced that Diddi's perfect musical ear was behind her talent for being able to communicate in so many languages. This musical talent was nurtured at Santiniketan and Diddi was among those who sang for the dance dramas that Tagore created. Their troupes were often taken to Calcutta to sing on air. From whatever I can gather of her time there, Diddi was a chatterbox, a person who made many friends and was always eager to take part in all of Tagore's experiments. Her photo albums have scores of photographs that document her life. Diddi and her friend carrying their holdall slung from a pole to their hostel. There are others that show Diddi chewing sugar cane, sitting on a bullock cart, on a barge with other students from Santiniketan when they accompanied Jean Renoir, the film-maker, to Banaras as he made his film on the Ganga. There are pictures of many who were to become iconic figures later—Satyajit Ray, Balraj Sahni, Mrinalini Sarabhai, Jaya Appaswami, Kanika Devi and Sankho Chaudhuri to name just a few. It must have been bliss to be in Santiniketan then and to be young and beautiful must have been very heaven.

Tagore's relationship with his students was inspirational in a way that is difficult for us to understand. It was something to do with the atmosphere of Santiniketan and its liberal teaching styles that brought out the best in all the students who came under its spell. Till the end, Diddi's face would light up at the mere mention of Santiniketan and a part of her remained forever the child she was when she first met Tagore.

In those days, Almora was also a sylvan retreat where several talented artists arrived to be inspired by its scenic landscape. Uday Shankar, the renowned dancer and elder brother of the legendary sitar player Ravi Shankar, had set up a dance academy just outside Almora. Its members included exotic foreign women, dancers and musicians and the estate came to be regarded as the Bohemian quarter of Almora. While the toffee-nosed Brahmin families guarded their daughters from its cosmopolitan culture, Diddi and Jayanti, because of their Santiniketan connection, were frequent visitors. They were often called upon to help in sourcing costumes and jewellery for the operas that Uday Shankar composed. Every summer, Tagore would travel to the hills and, whenever he came to Almora, he was a regular visitor to Kasoon. He stayed in a small hotel in the main town, called The Deodars, and since he was accompanied by his granddaughter, who was Diddi's friend, Diddi spent as much of her time with them as possible. She would take folk singers to Tagore and some of the tunes he composed were no doubt inspired by the pahari folksongs that he had heard in Almora.

Diddi's years at Santiniketan are recalled in a small book she wrote sometime in the early sixties. Called *Amader Santiniketan* (My Santiniketan), it is among her finest works. The following article, not from the book, is a piece she published on her favourite teacher there—the famous Hindi and Sanskrit scholar Acharya Hajari Prasad Dwivedi. I have chosen this essay over an extract from *Amader Santiniketan* because it captures the spirit of Santiniketan and Diddi's response to its romantic atmosphere so vividly.

~

How Can I Forget?

Diddi writes:

I first met Acharya Hajari Prasad Dwivedi in 1935: I was twelve years old and he a teacher at Santiniketan. For the next eight years, he was my teacher, guide, confidante—a guru in the truest sense of the word. When I shut my eyes to remember those halcyon days, I see silken curtains lift and a stage in my mind's eye. I am back in the Ashram, and a part of the audience that awaits the opening of a play.

I can see the wide swathe of red earth that separated the Ashram from a vast dusty field. On the far side of the field lies Gurupalli—where the gurus of the Ashram lived. Covered with creepers and lined with tall palms, they stand in a neat row like dolls' houses. The largest of these modest mud and thatch cottages belonged to the 'Big Guru', Hajari Prasad Dwivedi. It was a clean, spartan space, like its occupants, and was flanked by two verandas. In one corner of the front veranda lay a wooden divan, and in the other stood a battered wooden cupboard, tilting drunkenly on one broken foot, with books tumbling out in a heap. The back of the house had another veranda facing a courtyard and a small kitchen leading off from it. This was Panditji's wife's domain and Bhabhi (as we all called her affectionately) would rustle up good North Indian food for all of us non-Bengali students who missed our homes. Soon this house became our adda, a favourite hangout for all who wanted to eat spicy snacks. Bhabhi added onions, chillies and mustard oil to puffed rice and placed a whole heap before us, watching us fondly as we fell upon it with cries of delight.

Panditji, with his dhoti, loose khadi kurta and a shawl thrown carelessly over his shoulders, was a familiar figure in the Ashram. Tall, with a high forehead and twinkling eyes hidden behind a pair of glasses, he was best known for his spontaneous and open laughter that would erupt at the slightest provocation and ring out over the Ashram.

Panditji's style of teaching was pretty unique too. He told us hilarious stories of his teachers and at the first hint of a raindrop, he would dismiss the class for the day. I must break off to tell you that Santiniketan was the only school in the world where students were given a holiday to soak themselves the day it rained. So whenever it rained, shrieks of delight could be heard all over the campus as bands of students danced and sang noisily in the rain.

To go back to Panditji's classes: apart from the rainy day holiday, he offered us a host of other excuses to run away from

61

class. Fetch me some blades (or soap) for shaving, he would tell one and the delighted student would trot off happily to the Ashram's lone cooperative store. Since there was always a little something for the volunteer at the end of such an errand, often the whole class obliged Panditji by accompanying the lucky student. Yet, like all placid people, when his temper was roused it was an occasion to remember. For some unknown reason, someone had introduced a new fad into the Ashram those days: sucking the stone of an amla. All over the Ashram, you could see mouths working round the delectable amla stones. Panditji, like all the other Ashram gurus, had warned us to stop, but has any reasonable plea ever worked on schoolchildren?

One of the most timid boys in our class was Sharan Prasad. One day, Panditji caught him crunching the offending stones. 'So this is what you come here for? To crunch these wretched stones?' he thundered. 'How many are there in that mouth? Open it!' he ordered. Sharan Prasad quickly hid the one he was sucking under his tongue and opened his mouth.

'Hmmm,' said Panditji. 'Don't think you can hide it from me. It's under your tongue, isn't it? Go stand in that corner for the rest of the period. Shame on you,' he went on. 'Look at her,' he pointed to me. 'She has just come from the hills and see how quietly and obediently she listens to every word. And look at you! Been here for God know how long, but it's made no difference to you, it seems.'

I was so chuffed at this praise in front of the whole class that had turned by now to stare at me that I choked. A violent coughing fit ensued and, with it, out popped the stone I had hidden under my tongue. It landed neatly at Panditji's feet. He looked a little nonplussed for a while and then burst into a loud guffaw. My ears still ring at the sound of that generous shout of laughter. His laughter shamed me more that day than a shout would have.

Another scene: we are all sitting with Panditji under the sky, and he is reading the 'Sundar Kand' of the Ramayana. When his deep baritone reads the text, everything seems so easy that there are no questions to ask. We listen entranced to the story of Lord Rama's exploits with the same attention that we listen to Abanindranath Tagore's Galper Class (Class for Storytelling). The most boring textbook prescribed in Panditji's course was a selection of poems that nobody (least of all Panditji) wanted to ever tackle. 'Why do you want me to read you this?' he would ask us. 'Read it by yourselves at home.'

'But Panditji,' I begged one day, 'who can we go to ask when we don't understand something? You have to help us—what will we do in the exams next month?'

'Stupid child,' he shook his head at me. 'What is there in it to ask?'

I still remember the lines and I am sure he does too.

'Speak, O koel!

Spread some sweetness in my life…'

'Look,' he clucked at me, 'we are talking here of a koel, a cuckoo, not a crow. Obviously it had a sweet voice and that is what must have pleased the poet. Got it? Enough, now vamoose! Class over!' What could I possibly say to him after this? But this same Panditji became a tyrant when he took lessons in Hindi grammar. He would make us slog for hours until we got it right.

'If you sleep through this class,' he warned us, 'you will never be able to write a line straight. Understand? This Gowra,' he suddenly turned to me one day. 'She was like a meek cow when she came here and look at her now! Don't think for a minute that I can't see what mischief you are up to,' he wagged a fat finger at me. 'I'll pull your ears out from your jaw one day! I am going to report you to Jayanti today, you watch!'

Thankfully, he carried out neither of these threats—my ears are intact nor did he report me to my elder sister Jayanti. And I can proudly say that I can remember every bit of the grammar that I learnt from him.

Often he would invite the whole class over to his home to stargaze. 'Go run, all of you,' he'd dismiss us. 'I have to meet Gurudev (or, I can't teach at this hour). Come after dark to my cottage—we'll hold our class there.' I don't know how teachers today would react to such unorthodox methods and timetables. But I tell you we loved it. We followed our gurus wherever they went like enchanted children behind a Pied Piper. That is why I cannot understand why we hear of students who hold demonstrations against their teachers and, worse, cheat at exams or threaten to stab them, and force them to retire before their time. Perhaps the definition of a guru is not the same as it was for us.

What will never change though is the memory of those mobile classes and those magical hours we spent stargazing with Panditji. He pointed out the stars to us, and one constellation after another took shape before our eyes. 'There is the Big Bear,' he said, tracing a circle with his thumb on a palm. He called it Sapt Rishi, the Seven Sages.

'Where, Panditji?'

'Arrey, this idiot Kusum can't see her own nose on her face. There, you ass!' he would point it out again.

Then he showed us the magical Milky Way. My little son recently told me how the Nainital Observatory had acquired the latest telescope. 'You know how huge it is?' he tried to tell me. I nearly laughed as I watched him struggle to explain. How could I puncture his earnest enthusiasm by telling him that the 'telescope' that had showed us the night sky was better than the best that money could buy. As Panditji pointed out one constellation after another, we were convinced that all the shining stars in the sky bowed as they introduced themselves to us, and became our friends for life. We had no telescope, no complicated instruments: just one crazy astronomer whose deep voice and expressive hands described the world of stars to us. Lost in the vastness of the sky and Panditji's stories, we often forgot the time, and remembered that we were hungry only when we heard the gong chime out the summons for dinner.

The next scene: a grammar class with Panditji. Today, he has brought Tagore's new novel *Char Adhyaye* to class. He read it aloud to us and this went on for several days. One day he came across the line *Deke ano Balukdangar Pandit Hajariprasad ke* (Go fetch Pandit Hajari Prasad Dwivedi from Balukdangar, the kindergarten) and guffawed over it for a long time. I must tell you about Panditji's guffaw.

Just as a jeweller knows the difference between a genuine and a cultured pearl, I can tell a heartfelt guffaw from a polite titter. The true guffaw rings out over the room and flows from the heart like a natural waterfall. And like the waterfall, it sprays all who stand near it with joy. Panditji had that kind of pure laugh. Perhaps it has changed now, but as far as I know, a true pearl does not age. Panditji's whole body would shake with mirth when he laughed. When his laughter floated over the Ashram, it spread a smile over every face. As our classes were held in the open air, every head would turn to his class at the sound of Panditji's guffaw. It was as if a multitude of bells tied to a single string were set in motion and a ripple of happiness ran through the entire Ashram.

'So, Kamla,' he said one day. 'I saw your brother wearing a red loincloth exercise at the crack of dawn today,' and roared with laughter. The rest of us laughed along with him, tickled to death at the thought of someone in a red loincloth doing his morning workout.

Panditji once decided to grow a beard and all of us got after him. 'Chhi, chhi, Panditji! It is disgusting. You look like some sadhu baba—you'll have to get rid of it!' Poor Panditji tried explaining that he had boils on his face that made shaving painful but no one was ready to hear any excuse. I smile as I remember how easy it was to bully him.

And this was a man regarded as a colossus in his field! I wonder what he made of this spoilt class that argued with him on the merits of a beard.

A few years ago, he took time from his busy lecture circuits to visit me. He was the same—the same delightful smile, the same shabby horn-rimmed glasses sliding down his nose. The only thing missing was his carelessly draped shawl. I had sent him a book I had written on Santiniketan and he had replied: 'I read the book you sent me. You have brought alive the Santiniketan days so vividly that they haunted me for a long while. Your little book has been able to paint a picture of the Ashram that many scholarly tomes have failed to do. You have the marvellous gift of bringing alive an era through personal anecdotes.'

That book never won any awards, although my publisher was sure it would win some important ones. Yet, believe me, that letter from Panditji means more to me than any award. His letter gave me the courage to write regularly and henceforth I never let any critical review or comment cow me down: Panditji's certificate gave me an armour that I wear proudly. Yet now as I sit down to paint a portrait of my guru, I feel curiously tongue-tied. A kaleidoscope of images flash past my eyes: Panditji rocking and reading the 'Sundar Kand'; roaring with laughter over the sight of Kamla's brother in a red loincloth at dawn; threatening to pull my ears from my jaw; Panditji's fat finger pointing out the stars to us. And now, there is another Panditji, one who wears a silk kurta and emerges from a sleek car. How do I focus my camera? Every good photographer looks for a good background before composing a portrait. My camera falters as I try to locate the one that I search for in vain: Panditji in his little thatched cottage in the Ashram, wearing crushed clothes and a shawl carelessly thrown over his shoulder. Under his armpit he carries an orange attendance register with Viswabharati stamped on it.

He had once written to me: 'How can I ever forget my students? All you little children stand eternally in front of me. How can I ever forget you? If I have been busy and not kept in touch, how can you say I have forgotten you?' Then he quoted me a poem of Tagore's:

'If a traveller cannot see the stars in the sky or the flowers that bloom along his path, can you say that he has forgotten them? They are the fragrance of his soul: they are the memories that fill his loneliness with joy. Is this forgetfulness?'

Gurupalli filled my soul with sweetness; its fragrance fills my loneliness with joy.

How can I ever forget you, Panditji?

4

Diddi and Babu

Diddi finished her BA from Viswabharati University in 1943 and returned to Almora: she had a BA honours degree in philosophy. This was soon after her father had died and the family had lost its money. In fact, the last year of her education at Santiniketan had been partly funded by my aunt Jayanti, who was teaching there, and partly by Hamid Bhai, an old family friend from Rampur, whom Diddi regarded as her true brother till his death in the late seventies.

The golden age of Kasoon was over and Ama battled hard to bring up her brood of children without any support from her relatives. There was a small pension from Rampur but how far that went is anyone's guess. I once asked Ama what was stored in a huge wooden chest in her room. 'Oh that,' she waved at it carelessly, 'that was for the silver vessels I was given when I got married.'

'Where are they now?' I asked. Ama laughed and pointed to her round stomach—'Here!' she twinkled. Only one silver thaal remained as a token from that collection, and her gods sat on it in the puja room.

My uncle Tribhi, himself barely out of Santiniketan, soon found himself a job in Tikamgarh as the private secretary to the maharaja of Orchcha and left Almora with his young bride. He had been recently married off to the sweet and submissive Kumaoni girl Daya, who Lohaniji had once been sent to approve and was my mother's lifelong friend and confidante. It was on her persuasion and partly because Diddi could not bear to burden her young brother's family with an additional presence that, within a year of her return from Santiniketan, she agreed to marry my father, a young widower called Shukdeo Pant.

The story of Diddi and Babu, as we called our father, is a labyrinth that is dark and full of shadows.

My father's first wife, Ganga, and the story of their love for each other could be straight out of an eighteenth-century romantic novel. He was a young and earnest student, terribly reserved and quiet. A brilliant student, he had topped the Allahabad University in chemistry and taken the ICS exam. Everyone expected him to sail through it but he did not make it and was forced to take up a job as a schoolteacher. Worse, he fell violently in love with a beautiful and spirited girl called Ganga. When he told his father he wanted to marry her, the heavens fell. Are you mad, his father exploded in anger. She has tuberculosis! In those days, TB was the scourge of Kumaon and there was hardly a house that had not been ruined by it. Those who could afford it moved the patient to a sanatorium to save the rest of the family but, invariably, such stories had tragic ends and there was virtually no Kumaoni family where a daughter or daughter-in-law had not lost her life to tuberculosis.

My father apparently rode out his father's anger and married Ganga anyway. They say she fainted at the wedding itself and was carried over the threshold in my father's arms. I try and imagine the stir this must have created in the Almora of those days. Husbands and wives were never allowed to show any affection for each other in public and touching your wife was

69

scandalous beyond belief. Within a year, they had a daughter, my half-sister Binu, and in a few months, Ganga was so ill that she was shifted to a sanatorium in Gethiya, near Nainital. However, neither my father's devoted nursing nor the doctors in the sanatorium could save her. Ganga died within two years of marrying Babu, leaving behind a small daughter. The child, named Veena, but always called Binu at home, was sent to live with her mother's family in Nainital and my grandfather began to pester my father to remarry. A winter's night and a man's youth, Diddi writes in 'Lati', stretch endlessly. Perhaps for this reason, or more probably because there was a small child to bring up, my father married Diddi in May 1945. My sister Mrinal was born exactly nine months later, in February 1946.

Typically, Diddi hardly ever spoke to us about why she submitted so tamely to a match that must have shaken her life. Nor did she ever speak of the hardships she must have endured as she and Babu came to terms with each other's personalities and she adjusted to life in a conservative Brahmin home. Babu's salary was pitiful and Diddi, never a careful housekeeper, struggled hard to make ends meet. Years later, when she had worked out the bitterness from her system, she told us funny anecdotes from those days. The hardships she reserved to narrate in her novels and stories.

Diddi went to Tikamgarh to be with her family when her first child was due. It was Ama who insisted that Binu be brought back from her grandparents and be brought up along with Diddi's own child so that the two would grow up together. Thus, Babu was sent to Nainital soon after he and Diddi were married to collect Binu from her grandparents. Years later, Diddi told me in a rare mood of confiding of a scene reported to her by someone who was travelling on the same train. Apparently, Babu was standing holding Binu's hand at the platform on Kathgodam waiting for the train to arrive. Binu was distracted by a basket of chickens that was to be loaded on the train and kept pointing to them to draw Babu's attention. Babu, however, stood looking at the far horizon, oblivious of the child tugging at his hand. His mind must have been seething with so much: painful memories of Ganga, fears of the future, despair at his financial condition. The unbearable poignancy of the scene haunts me, as it must have haunted Diddi and impelled her to tell me all those years later and in it, I think, lay Diddi's protective attitude to Binu. Till the very end of her life, Diddi would never gift Minu and me anything without gifting it first to Binu. In her will, she left a special bit for Binu alone and it speaks immensely of their mutual generosity that Binu promptly shared it among us all.

Binu was a sickly, rickety child and no wonder as her mother was almost riddled with TB when Binu was in her womb. Like any child, confused after being tossed from one house to another, she was sulky and wilful as well. A photograph in my mother's album shows Binu when was about five and Minu about three. Minu is happily cuddling a rabbit while Binu, dressed in an identical frock, wearing her mother's necklace with a bindi on her forehead, scowls into the camera. That photograph speaks volumes for the kind of tough task that Diddi had on her hands. 'Look Gaura,' Ama had told her, 'bringing up someone else's child is like trying to eat the flesh of your palm but promise me you will never make a difference between your own children and your stepchild.'

Diddi rose to the challenge and the whole Kasoon clan entered into a conspiracy of silence. Not only was Binu's mother's name never mentioned in our presence, I never saw a picture or heard of her until much, much later.

Soon after Minu was born, my parents moved to Nainital where Babu was appointed the chemistry teacher in the newly opened Birla Vidya Mandir, a public school set up by the Birla Educational Trust. Diddi's foster-sister, Munna, was by now the matron there and Diddi had her hands full with looking after two small girls and taking care of her father-in-law, who died soon after they came to Nainital. I arrived in 1951, and by then Babu had joined the government service and was back in Almora posted as the District Inspector of Schools. Three girls and a small salary—as if this was not enough to crush her spirit, there was the clash of two strong temperaments as Diddi and Babu adjusted to each other.

When I look back, it is so clear that the two of them were polar opposites in many matters: she was fun-loving, gregarious and outgoing. He was quiet, moody and introverted. She was a spendthrift, he careful with his money. She hated housework and the drudgery of the kitchen, and never sewed or embroidered. Babu, on the other hand, wanted her to be the kind of housewife that other women of her generation were— efficient and thrifty in household matters. Diddi loved meat and non-vegetarian food while Babu was a fastidious vegetarian. Diddi was fond of telling us that apart from a kite, she had eaten everything that flew and, but for a cot, everything with four legs. She chewed the bones and sucked at the marrow of the bones whenever meat was cooked, slyly watching the disgust on his face. She walked in the house with wooden clogs on— knowing that Babu was allergic to noise of any kind. He hated strong perfumes—Diddi loved burning incense sticks that you could smell from a mile. Violent arguments took place and ended in long silences. I think she took a peculiar pleasure in provoking him and would deliberately do all the things he most hated to prove that he could never, ever, crush her spirit. Oddly—or perhaps, predictably—she became a vegetarian after his death. She would still cook delicious kababs and meat curries for us, but would never touch a morsel of meat herself. No matter how tempted she was—she once told Minu that she could kill for a tin of sardines—she never broke that vow of abstinence she imposed on herself after Babu's death.

Despite their volatile rows and her deliberate defiance, Diddi's dependence on Babu was pathetic. A frown from him diminished her and no matter how much she grumbled and resisted his laws, she submitted to his will each time. Babu was the archetypal stoic: when faced with stress, he lapsed into a brooding silence. Looking back at our childhood, I can count scores of occasions when Babu would sink into one of his black moods, to remain silent and uncommunicative for days, weeks almost, and no one knew what had triggered it off. When that happened, we pussy-footed around him, ran away from any chance of an encounter and hid behind books and homework to avoid him and the thick atmosphere between our parents.

Diddi made it no easier by letting us know, without ever referring to the cause of Babu's mood, how miserable she was. She would go around with a red nose (and we privately called her Rudolf, after the red-nosed reindeer), with a tragic air of injured innocence. In the manner of all children who opt for desperate remedies, I remember wishing that one of them would die and then dream about the tragic consequences were that to happen, and imagine our heroic handling of it. To date, nothing upsets me more than a moody silence and my nervous chatter is a habit cultivated by the oppressive silences I have heard in my childhood. I was deeply envious of children whose parents were happy and spoke lovingly to each other, of those families that went on holidays together and of homes where money was not the cause of thick silences.

However, I can also now see how wrong it was of Diddi to load her misery on us, for even though she never spoke directly

73

of it, her unhappiness was evident to all of us. An offshoot of this was that Babu became a figure of fear to us children: a man to be kept at an arm's distance. We created our relationship with him by following the lead he showed us: if he was happy, we smiled; if he was silent, we kept out of his way. And how we looked forward to the times when he went out of town on a tour! As soon as Babu stepped beyond the gate, a collective whoop of joy would ring through the house. Someone would switch on the radio and put on loud film music, we would jump up and down on Babu's bed and heave a collective sigh of relief that the source of our tension had vanished. For the next few days, our house was full of fun and laughter. All this ended as soon as it was time for him to return from his tour. Years later, when I saw the film *Sound of Music* for the first time, I understood perfectly the terror that Christopher Plummer struck in the hearts of his children. Unfortunately, my mother was no Julie Andrews and contributed substantially to isolating Babu from his children. I can now see him as a lonely man, unable by his taciturn nature to come close to us or participate in our childhood. His moody silence was a concession of defeat to a woman whose vivacious personality and quick wit had granted him the respect of his children but left him out of the circle of love they shared with their mother.

Our attitude to Babu changed radically after we were married and visited Lucknow where he and Diddi spent their last years together. He was gentle and soft-spoken as always but also so tolerant of the noise generated by his high-spirited grandchildren that we had to pinch ourselves to remember that this was the father who hated us thumping up and down the wooden staircase at Priory Lodge. Now there were conversations between us and he enjoyed listening to our funny stories about our husbands and their families. Diddi and he were closer than we had ever seen them and she had become a devoted wife. When he was diagnosed with cirrhosis of the liver—after a bad bout of hepatitis—she nursed him uncomplainingly and was all alone when he died. She rang up the relatives to inform them of his death and organized the money that would take care of the expenses of the funeral rites.

In their last years, my parents were inseparable. Diddi no longer itched to go visit her mother and her Kasoon relatives and Babu's support for, and quiet pride in, her writing meant more to her than we ever realized. When her children left to live their own lives, Diddi surrendered herself totally to Babu. And after his death, whenever she spoke of him it was with such love and respect that I often wondered whether I was wrong in remembering her Rudolf days. All his eccentricities and moodiness were now funny stories that she told our children— there was no trace of bitterness or any anger at all. My niece, Radhika, once brought a form for eye donation and asked Diddi to sign up. 'Nonsense!' Diddi replied. 'If I die and go sightless to heaven, how on earth will I find Babu? Suppose I cosy up to the wrong buddha!'

Then, I remembered a short story, called 'Band Ghari' (The clock that stopped working) that she had written in the early sixties, when we were at Priory Lodge. It has a thinly disguised autobiographical character, Maya, possibly Diddi herself. I could not trace the story until Binu located it for me in an old collection of her short stories and sent it across, long after I had completed this chapter. However, I knew immediately that it had to be included because it brings out the relationship that Babu and Diddi shared so clearly. More importantly, it mirrored my memories of Priory Lodge and the heavy atmosphere I remember so clearly even after so many decades that it was gratifying to know that I was not completely wrong in my assessment of that time. Babu's moods, his sudden and inexplicable temper eruptions and the joy that we all felt when he went on a tour—all these are described by Diddi in moving, but humorous, detail.

So by the time I put the finishing touches to this chapter it was evident to me that Diddi came to acknowledge a fundamental truth about Babu after he died: that her birth as a writer was prompted by Babu's personality. She had embarked on her writing career as a defiant gesture against the suffocating laws of his family. Yet, as her popularity grew, she became more famous than him. Alarmed at this wholly new reversal of roles, she not only underplayed her place in the world, she tried hard to include his contribution in whatever she had achieved. For she knew—as her mother did too—that if Babu had left her to run wild, as my aunt Jayanti's husband had done, Diddi would have become a charming eccentric who told delightful tales and nothing more. Ama once told Binu that Diddi was like a spirited filly: 'It was only your father,' she told Binu, 'who could control her.'

This is why, after Babu died in 1974, Diddi was completely devastated. For the first time in her life, she was left without a guiding male presence and she realized how valuable his steadying presence had been both in creating her into a responsible woman and giving the children a set of laws within which to develop their talents. In an article she wrote on him soon after he died, Diddi paid him a tribute that came straight from her heart. I reproduce just the opening of that article for not only is it very painful to see her naked sorrow as it develops, its idiom is difficult to reproduce in English without marring it. Yet it showed me clearly what I never understood when I saw Diddi and Babu inflict each other with cruelty in my childhood—that she loved him deeply and was dependent on him in a way we never understood. That without Babu, there would have been no Diddi.

~

Babu

Part of the article Diddi wrote on Babu's death (1974):

Where shall I start? From that balmy spring evening when he came to our haveli in Orchcha, which was festooned with garlands of mango-leaves and glittering with lights? Riding an elephant as he led the wedding procession, he was greeted at the gates by the court singers, Idiya and Koel. The evening hummed with the music of the traditional bannas as they welcomed my bridegroom.

Shall I start with the first time he held my hand? Or with the day before his death, when he heard me weep quietly in the dark and groped to hold my hand in a silent goodbye? My pen hovers between the two memories. The first one recalls the joy with which I agreed to abide by all the rules of a good Hindu wife among the chant of the Sanskrit mantras. The second takes me cruelly to the cold, hard steps of the Sati Ghat in Haridwar to remind me where that journey ended and I stood alone under the sultry monsoon sky looking at the serene waters of the Ganga.

I climb down the steps and wade waist deep into the cool waters of the river. Our family priest, Pandit Hariramji, avoids my eyes as his deep voice asks me to take a handful of the holy waters and say *'Chitadahashamanartham'*—with this water, I cool the embers of your funeral pyre. However hard I try, I cannot erase the sight of the funeral pyre and his body burning on it.

My lips can hardly mumble the words.

Another bullet is ready to pierce my ears. As Hariramji goes on with the chants, he suffixes *pret* (spirit) to the name that I loved above all. A dagger twists itself into my heart each time and I turn my gaze away from him and it falls on my son. His young face is steeped in a sadness he can hardly comprehend as he repeats the mantras after the priest. Each line hammers one nail after another into our hearts.

It is time now for molten glass to be poured into our ears. 'Take all his everyday belongings and throw them into these waters,' we are told. My son bends to pick them from a bundle at our feet and I watch each one float away as it is dropped into the flowing river. The last to bob away are his spectacles. They raise their head from the waters and the sunlight glints on one lens as it tries to catch my eye, then gives up and quietly sinks.

Across the river are the Shivalik hills and behind them the sky stretches in an endless sweep. The sound of the river and the waves lapping against our wet bodies come with one message: you are no more what you were. You are alone, looted of all your wealth, your identity. No woman can be given a harsher punishment than widowhood, can she?

For me, his death has robbed me of not just a mate, a spouse but my finest reader, my most honest critic.

~

Band Ghari

A short story by Diddi (early 1960s):

Maya lifted the green curtains in Chaya Jiji's house and peered out—she could hardly see anything through the panes frosted over with moisture. A dense mist had smothered everything outside and all that was visible was the twinkle of street lights shining intermittently though the swirling moisture like glow-worms. A sharp clap of thunder announced ominously that a strong downpour was on its way any minute now. 'Jiji still hasn't finished her rounds at the hospital,' Maya thought. 'Who knows when another expectant mother may decide to go into labour? The children must have come back from school by now.' She dropped the curtain with an irritated twitch of her hand and called Jiji's khansama. 'Tell Jiji I came,' she told him. 'Tell her I waited a long time for her—I'll come again tomorrow.'

She stepped out into the clawing mist and fumbled her way homewards, cursing her sister who had let her down once again. She had been dying to see *Love in the Afternoon* and Jiji had let her down. There is just one more day of freedom left before the chains would be back on her ankles, she calculated, for Girish was returning on Wednesday. Let's hope she can come tomorrow, Maya thought, and that some patient doesn't mess up our plans.

Her house was ablaze with lights—the drawing room ones as well. A chill wind enveloped Maya's thudding heart—O God, did this mean that he had returned earlier than he was supposed to? As soon as she let herself in, Sonia came running to her. 'Mummy,' she whispered conspiratorially, winding her little arms round her mother's knees, 'Papa is back from his tour and his mood is terrible! This terrible,' she spread her little hands wide to show her mother how much. 'Know what, Mummy,' she went on, 'he said, "Son of a pig" to the driver and...'

'All right, enough,' Maya shushed her hurriedly and disentangled herself.

Suddenly, the bathroom door burst open and a lion emerged. 'So, you are back, are you?' the lion asked. 'Here I come through storms and blizzards, driving across mountains and valleys in a jeep and what do I find? No wife, not even a cup of tea! So why don't you go out again and have some more fun?' His cruel eyes pinioned her where she stood.

'I hadn't gone anywhere special—just to Chaya Jiji's,' Maya replied as calmly as she could and put her bag down with trembling hands.

'Very kind of you, I'm sure,' Girish spat at her and settled down with the newspaper.

Maya turned to go to the kitchen, hot tears of anger and humiliation blinding her as she groped her way. 'Mummy, Mummy,' two-year-old Atul clung to her, followed by Rostry, their Alsatian. Rostry's tail waved so vigorously when he saw his mistress that it knocked over a huge brass flower pot and it keeled over with a resounding crash. Girish lowered his newspaper and kicked Rostry aside, 'Get out, you stupid hound,' he yelled. 'Can't a man expect two minutes of peace in this benighted house?'

A deathly hush fell over everyone, including the slinking dog. The ayah came and scooped up Atul, muttering, 'Is the sahib a bomb or what?' to herself. Maya locked herself into the bathroom and Sonia took out a rough notebook and started drawing hideous faces in it. She wrote 'Papa is a devil' under the first one. The next one, an even more frightening monster face, had 'Papa is a big fat devil' under it. At this point, Pratul returned from his friend's place, where he had gone to hear some pop music. He entered, wearing a new pair of tight drainpipe trousers, humming and whistling *Lipstick on your coh-a-llar*, his eyes blind to Girish behind the newspaper. Suddenly, his eyes fell on the brass flower pot on the floor and his horrified gaze turned to the chair where his father sat looking at him coldly.

'Akkhha, welcome, Prince of Wales,' Girish greeted him, smiling through tight lips. 'So how many films have you seen? Is this wonderful song about lipstick from some new Hollywood hit?'

'N-no, papa,' the poor boy stammered. 'It is from the Binaca Hit Parade.'

'Of course, of course,' Girish went on in the same voice. 'Your poor father toils and sweats his life away so that he can hear his beloved son whistle *Lipstick on your collar* to him! Go,' he thundered, 'change out of these effeminate trousers immediately and wear something decent. How dare you whistle in front of your father? And obscene tunes like the one you just did? Bring your maths books and come back here! At your age, I used to recite Chakravarti's algebra, not these obscene songs! I wish you knew your sixteen times tables as well as you know these Binaca Hit Parade tunes. I just don't understand what we pay the school for! Useless teachers and even more useless students! These are the times we live in!'

Pratul quietly left the room to change his trousers.

Girish Chandra Sharma was the most respected and renowned engineer of the irrigation department. He was entrusted with the task of creating new roads in the most difficult mountain areas and his skill at using dynamite to blast new pathways was well known. He ran his department with an iron hand and drove everyone hard by setting an example of unflinching devotion to duty. His attitude towards his family was no different, yet he was unable to see how his strict discipline had gnawed away whatever love his children had for him. This was why whenever he went on a tour, the house burst into a frenzy of celebrations. Maya would dump Atul with the ayah and go off to her sister's. The two of them would gossip for hours and when she came back after sunset to her own house,

Maya wished her life was as uncluttered as Chaya Jiji's. How lucky her sister was! No fractious children, no tetchy husband and black moods to deal with. And Chaya would think enviously of all that her sister had—three loving children and a handsome husband. I wish I was Maya, she would sigh. Chaya was plainer than Maya but what a brain she had! Maya, on the other hand, was pretty but had none of her sister's self-confidence. Both the sisters had been brought up by their father, a renowned surgeon, and surrounded by love in their childhood. Maya was the spoilt one and her father had taken special care to choose a husband worthy of his pretty, but spoilt, younger daughter. His eye had fallen on Girish, a brilliant student who had just passed out of the Roorkee Engineering College with flying colours.

Girish knew that his father-in-law respected his brilliance but had made it very clear to his wife that he would never be overawed by her rich and spoilt childhood. Both stood their ground, and whenever they argued, which was often, neither would yield an inch to the other. Maya would get emotional and tearful and Girish hated tears and tantrums. She loved bright colours but Girish would dampen her efforts immediately by saying something cutting. 'If you had killed a mouse and painted your mouth with its blood, you might look even better,' he once told her after she had put on some lipstick. Maya thought that bliss was nothing compared to gnawing at a leg of roast chicken and Girish was a strict vegetarian. If meat was ever served, he would leave the table and pretend he was too nauseated to finish his meal.

Chaya was quite adept at extracting information from Maya. 'This is the limit!' she once said to a tearful Maya. 'Is he a father or a monster? I'm going to speak to him tomorrow.' Yet, secretly, she also knew that her sister's relationship with her husband had a deep undercurrent of passion and that their sparring was part of the game of love that they played between themselves.

For his part, Girish could not stand his sister-in-law. Ever since she had been transferred to the same town, he felt he had lost his wife to her. Their conversations were now reduced to grunts and monosyllables, and the iron hand of his discipline became even more pronounced to protect his turf from his sister-in-law's constant intrusions. The result was that everyone forgot what it was like to laugh and joke and mealtimes were a trial. Ordinary arguments between the two became full-fledged wars and the children lost their sparkle. They now resembled toys that have been displayed for too long in a shop window. As the tensions of the house grew, they began to spill outside it. Memsahib would pick on the servants and sahib made life hell for everyone in the office: the clerks and peons trembled in their shoes whenever Girish summoned them.

It was March—a month when all the accounts of the department had to be submitted to the government auditors; there were bills and files piled all over the office. And to top it all, Girish's wife and children had shut him out of their lives. He realized the sympathies of the children lay with their mother and this made him madder still. Stung, he made life hell for everyone in the house. If the cook had made parathas for dinner, he would ask for a phulka; he hated moong dal but now would have nothing but watery moong dal every day. Thalis would fly off the table if the food was not to his liking and glasses flung if the water was not cool or warm enough. Maya, for her part, would answer by clanging pots and pans in the kitchen. Her frustration and irritation manifested itself in the angry clatter of tongs and ladles. Matters finally reached such a head that the entire home seemed in imminent danger of being swept away on the tide of their anger.

Then, one day, as Maya was unfolding a packet of turmeric

to put away in a bottle, her eye fell upon the newspaper packet that the grocer had put the spice in. 'Death of a twenty-year-old woman' read the headline. 'Fed up with the constant bickering and domestic violence in her home, twenty-year-old Mrs Kher poured a bottle of kerosene oil and set herself aflame.' Maya reread the news item: a minute of pain and then bliss forever from the eternal squabbling for Mrs Kher, she thought. Her eyes shone with excitement as she resolved to do exactly what that poor suffering woman had had the courage to do. That'll teach Girish a lesson, she thought spitefully. Serve him right if he has to take care from now on of the dhobi and milk accounts. I'd like to see how he runs this house on the meagre allowance he gives me. Let's see what he does if Atul gets up in the middle of the night burning with fever. But the mere thought of little Atul suffering weakened her resolve: Atul was her darling and every night he groped to hold the gold chain round her throat before he drank milk from his bottle. If she wasn't there he wouldn't sleep. She came back late from Chaya's house one day and Atul threw such a tantrum that he developed a fever as a result. Sonia has to be hugged before she goes to school and bribed with small change to buy something for herself from the tuckshop. And her spoilt brat, Pratul! He claims to get constipated unless he reads comics in the loo, so Maya has to run her house on a deficit budget to buy him ten comics every month. As for Girish himself, for all his screeching and shouting, is there anyone but Maya who can pacify him?

To hell with all of them, she thought defiantly. Her chest swelled with pride as she made up her mind and then tears filled her eyes as she imagined her death scene. Sonia will come back from school and not see her beloved mummy at the tea table with fresh snacks made for her. Her horrified eyes will go to the floor where her mother's body lies covered by a shroud.

The culprit Girish will be slumped in a chair and little Atul will throw his arms round her inert body and lisp, 'Geth up, Mummy.' At this point Girish will burst into an uncontrollable fit of weeping and beat his chest wailing, 'Why have you punished me, Maya? Why?'

Maya smiled to herself as she collected a bottle of kerosene oil on her way to the bathroom. Then suddenly she remembered the new olive-green Kanjeevaram sari that Chaya Jiji had just gifted her. She hadn't worn it even once! Shouldn't she wear it for a last time today before she died? Maya washed her face, put on her new sari, tied her hair in an attractive bun and carefully put a pretty bindi. She looked at herself with the eyes of a martyr in the mirror and fell in love with what she saw there. I wish I could see Atul just once more, she said and tiptoed quietly to the drawing room. Atul was sitting there by himself and rolling a round box of boot polish on the floor. Rostry would run and pick it up and bring it back to his little master and the game would start again. Atul clapped his hands in glee each time his trusty dog came back with the box. Maya's eyes filled up at this happy scene, but she steeled herself and tiptoed away. This time she must not falter in her resolve, she thought, and she picked up the bottle of kerosene oil and a box of matches and turned towards the bathroom. 'Mummy,' Pratul had said this morning as he went to school, 'I need a fresh white shirt for this evening's school debate. Please sew that missing button for me, will you?' She pulled out the wretched shirt and sat down to put the missing button in. Little would anyone know that this was the last button she ever sewed on for anyone, she thought. Her eyes filled up again and she could hear Atul's little hands clap and his gurgle of laughter as Rostry and he played their little game. She must stop this, she had to lock herself into the bathroom and...I can't burn this beautiful Kanjeevaram sari, she thought. They could give it to Sonia when she got married. Why don't I pull out some old sari and wear that instead? Maya drew a deep breath and got up once more when her ears pricked up as they heard the unexpected sound of Girish's laughter. 'What is this, you rascal? Have you seen your face, you monkey? Ha ha ha...' She had yearned for so long to hear it that she had almost forgotten what it was like to hear him laugh. 'Oh, my word! I can't believe this...' Girish's voice went on and another guffaw followed.

'Why, what has he done, Papa?' Sonia and Pratul ran and then the sound of delighted laughter rang through the house. Maya threw the bottle away and ran to see what had happened. The clock showed two in the afternoon—damn! Had it stopped? She took it close to her ear and, sure enough, there was no tick-tock to be heard. The children and Girish had come back from school and the office and she hadn't even got the tea going, she realized. At this point, her family walked into the room in a curious procession. Perched on his father's shoulders was little Atul, behind them were Sonia and Pratul and the rear was brought up a grinning Rostry, his tail waving wild circles of delight.

It was as if an overcast sky was suddenly pierced by bright sunshine and Maya's sad face lit up at what she saw. Mr Atul Kumar Sharma, his face painted with circles of black boot polish, wore a huge grin that displayed both his teeth to his admiring audience. Maya looked at her husband's face and silently held out a treaty. As soon as he saw his mother, Atul began to fidget to reach her. Maya spread her arms wide to receive him and accidentally touched her husband's shoulder.

Girish quietly pinched her arm, unseen by the children. 'Oof,' she said in mock anger and began to kiss Atul. 'How foolish Chaya Jiji is!' she thought silently. 'She calls my husband an

86

unfeeling bastard. If only she could see him now, she'd never say this again.'

'What time is it, Sonia?' said Girish. 'I have a meeting at quarter past four.'

Sonia ran to see the clock. 'O Papa,' she came back laughing, 'this clock is a gone case. Do you know what time it says? Two o'clock!'

Maya looked at the clock in gratitude. She felt that there could be nothing more beautiful in the world than the stilled hands on its face.

5

Priory Lodge

My brother, Muktesh, was born in Almora in 1954. The joy and happiness that his birth brought to my parents is a distinct memory even though I was just three at the time. He was born in the afternoon and Tara Didi, Ama's Sancho Panza, came running in to announce the great tidings to the waiting family. Ama blew a conch shell to thank the gods for finally giving my mother a son, and Tara Didi caught hold of me and smashed a lump of jaggery on my back in gratitude for bringing a brother behind me. From that day on, my brother was everyone's favourite child.

A few months later, Babu was transferred to Lucknow and we left Almora to go to the plains. It was our family's first step outside the secure cocoon of the mountains and the Kasoon clan.

Lucknow is a hazy memory: I remember a small flat in River Bank Colony, hot summer nights spent on the terrace and the desolate ruins of the Residency that we could see from our balcony. Then, Babu was sent by the government to Canada and the US on a study trip and for the first time since she was married, Diddi got a chance to be herself without Babu or her Kasoon family to cramp her style. It was roughly around this time that Diddi started writing short stories under the pseudonym of Shivani—a synonym of her name, Gaura. She also took up occasional work with the All India Radio, often gave talks, and wrote features and radio plays. Binu was sent to learn music at the Bhatkhande Academy and Minu to learn Bharatanatyam. I was enrolled at La Martiniere's School for Girls and it pleased Diddi no end that all of us excelled at all these various places. Binu sang so beautifully that she was often on air on children's programmes and Minu was the star performer at her school. So in the year that Babu was away in Canada Diddi quickly started off what she had been itching to do for a while: give her children a taste of life beyond school and the family.

River Bank Colony was a U-shaped complex of flats and we soon got accustomed to living within earshot of our neighbours' lives. After the isolated life in the cantonment house in Almora and the noisy family at Kasoon, living in such close proximity to families that we were not related to was a new and exciting experience. The flat on our left was shared by three bright young women—Leela Khazanchand, Leela Joseph and Sushmi Matthews. Leela Khazanchand's father was our family doctor in Almora and later the director of the famous Bhowali Sanitorium; Leela Joseph taught at the Mahila College; and Sushmi Matthews was a senior scientist at the Central Drug Research Institute. Their flat was full of comings and goings and had an aquarium with goldfish that fascinated me. Sushmi Diddi nicknamed my brother Micky and we kept in touch with them for several years later. In the flat on the other side lived the Chaturvedi family, many brothers who were doctors and an old mother everyone called Chachi. Sandwiched between them, Diddi's family swung its eyes from one house to another as if a giant tennis match was in progress. One of the Chaturvedi doctors fell in love with one of the young girls on the other side and Chachi went into convulsions over the prospect of Christian blood polluting her pure Brahmin bloodline. Upstairs was a family where someone played the sitar and Diddi named them Da-da-da-dyaoon after the scales that hit the air each morning. Diddi's fertile mind constantly filed away incidents, characters and romances and she revelled in the rich lode of stories that life in River Bank Colony provided her. For years she would use these days as plots or characters.

We came to Nainital in 1958, a return to Kumaon after four years in Lucknow. Our new home was called Priory Lodge, a huge gothic pile with so many rooms that I don't think anyone ever counted them. One part of the house was ours and the rest belonged to Babu's office that smelt of old files, wood smoke from the sigris to warm the clerks, and their bidis. Diddi found out that it had once been run as a club by an old Englishwoman and she and her khansama had died in a fire that broke out. Sometimes, Diddi claimed, she came with her khansama to walk over her old rooms and had been spotted by our servants. She promptly christened this resident spook Miss Perry, after a particularly strict teacher in my brother's school who used to beat the boys with a feather duster.

Priory Lodge was situated in a thickly wooded area of Nainital called Ayarpata where Jim Corbett once lived. His old house, Guerney House, was close by and a cemetery with tumbledown graves dating from the Raj was my favourite Saturday afternoon haunt. With a makeshift broom made of twigs and branches, I used to sweep the old graves and place flowers on them, much to Diddi's amusement. Like all old cemeteries, this one, too, had its share of sorrowful epitaphs—a child who had died in infancy; a young officer who was done in by the tropical climate of India; and a whole family of missionaries, whose graves lay in a cluster at the far end. All around our house were the estates of the erstwhile royal families of Uttar Pradesh and Diddi was delighted to be surrounded once more by the kind of life that she had seen in her childhood. Her novels and short stories of the time now had characters that present a vignette of life in the hill stations in the fifties, when India had just become a republic and the old princely states were disbanded. The estates had names such as Vienna Lodge, The Retreat, Fern Cottage, Strawberry Lodge, Ellesmere and The Hive. They lay shut most of the year and came to life when the 'season' started in May. Suddenly, the hills came alive with exotic people from the plains who came to their summer retreats to escape the dreadful heat of the North Indian plains.

Vienna Lodge had an old dowager maharani whose companion, Miss Brown, and private secretary, Mr Joshi, were characters straight out of a Raj film. Diddi became friends with them and we soon gained access to the library at Vienna Lodge. Mr Joshi once gave me the *Complete Works of Somerset Maugham* as a gift and my brother a beautiful wooden box of oil paints. Below their estate on the same hill was The Retreat where a Rana family came from Nepal every summer.

Their house remained as quiet as a tomb all morning and came alive from about noon, when the Rana awoke from his drink-induced stupor. Bright young maids, perhaps his concubines, fluttered around him like butterflies as they massaged his limbs and fed him his breakfast from a huge silver thali in the sunny forecourt. We would hang shamelessly from our veranda that overlooked their lawn and watch the tableau that was being enacted on the facing hill. Above Priory Lodge was Fern Cottage and a ferocious Sikh grandee, called Tikka Raja, took residence here in summer. He had hooded, puffy eyes and his face twitched constantly, making it even more

91

grotesque. Once, when he came to call on my parents, we were summoned to the drawing room and a fit of giggles broke out among us as he turned to us, his face twitching in all directions. 'What charming and pretty daughters you have,' he told Diddi. 'Always smiling—I like that. My sons are always scowling!' If only he knew the source of our smiles!

Every evening, these exotic neighbours would dress to their teeth, the men in expensive suits and their wives in glittering jewels and silks and chiffons. They would then be loaded into their *dandies* (litters that were carried on the shoulders of their liveried staff) and wind their way down to the Boat House Club, to drink, play cards and drink again. How we longed to go there ourselves but, of course, our parents were different. So while everyone went to the flats to hear the band that played lilting music that floated up in tantalizing snatches on the wind that blew across the lake, we sat over our books. Babu disapproved of going down to the town except once a week. And none of us dared to challenge his writ.

My aunt Jayanti's sons, Pushpesh and Muktesh, came to live with us in the early sixties and the six of us still believe that the time we spent together at Priory Lodge then was the most delightful time of our lives. Diddi ran her house pretty much like Ama ran Kasoon. Much to my father's chagrin, the run of the house was given to the servants while Diddi wrote stories and novels she read out aloud to us each evening. Babu's office had a vast collection of old journals and back issues of *The Listener* and the old *Kumaon Gazette* and they provided us with hours of reading material. Thankfully, we were all voracious readers and devoured everything that came our way and something about the liveliness that accompanied Diddi wherever she set up camp encouraged us to write and perform plays, bring out house magazines and become the epicentre of the neighbourhood's cultural life. Almora, Kasoon, the mad aunts and uncles soon receded from our childhood and significantly, even though Almora is a mere two hours from Nainital by road, we never once visited it in all the sixteen years we were in Nainital. The umbilical cord was snapped firmly and we were now on our own.

What I remember most from that time was a lack of money—Diddi herself had two sets of saris for going out and a couple more for everyday wear. We had our school uniforms and two sets each. We read from second-hand books in school and made our shoes last as long as they could before we dared to ask Babu for a new pair. I was so accustomed to hand-me-downs that I soon accepted that school textbooks would be handed down from cousins and friends and only in special cases could we ask for a new set. Most of my textbooks, thus, came down to me from yobs who lavishly added rude margin notes and lewd illustrations. I tried hard to cover my dog-eared textbooks by keeping them wrapped in clean brown-paper covers. One incident from that time still makes me laugh. Our Hindi textbook had a poem by the well-known poet Sumitranandan Pant. I was asked one day by my Hindi teacher, Miss Sood, who knew my mother wrote in Hindi, 'Ira, is Sumitranandan Pant a relative of yours?' Since my name was Pant and I was aware that almost all Pants, Pandes and Joshis were related to each other, I looked into the open book in front of me: whoever had used it before me had added a bindi and earrings to a hideous sketch of the poor poet, known for the effeminate ringlets he sported. It was impossible to tell the sex now, so I assayed a wild guess. 'Yes,' I replied confidently. 'She is my aunt.' Diddi had a good laugh when I told her about it and related this story to everyone who came home. In fact, it became a kind of party piece and I was asked to narrate it, mimicking Miss Sood's voice, to guests, who always roared with laughter at the punchline. By picking out the absurd and teaching me to laugh at it, she inoculated me from any false sense of shame at not being as rich as the rest of my schoolmates. It was a lesson I never forgot.

All around Priory Lodge were the summer cottages of the rich and privileged. We saw their lavish lifestyles from our veranda and created stories around these glimpses into another world. Yet I cannot recall being ashamed of what we did not have. On the other hand, since we all did outstandingly well at school, we had a healthy contempt for those who had rich parents but miserably boring lives. Their neat houses had no resident spooks and, above all, they did not have a mother like Diddi. In fact, parents from the neighbouring houses sent their children to our house every evening when Diddi sat with us over our homework. Diddi could make the most boring lessons interesting: she had stories about characters in history that fixed them permanently in our minds; devised clever sutras to help us learn dates and timelines; and helped us with our compositions and essays. Even later, when she came to visit us, her grandchildren used to ask her to help out with their holiday homework. One of the children had to once write an essay in Hindi on 'The autobiography of a crow' and just could not get started. It was Diddi who suggested that she try a variation of the Ugly Duckling story and make one up on how this crow was a foundling left by a koel in a crow's nest and how it always puzzled her that her voice was so different from that of her siblings. Thrilled with this tip, the child wrote a great essay and was rewarded later for it. Diddi supervised all our school work except maths. Maths was Babu's domain and how we dreaded those sessions. I wonder why, though, for he never raised his voice and, unlike Diddi, never smacked us. Yet something about him so pulverized my brain that I would get the easiest problems wrong.

94

The children's room—a huge draughty hall on the other side of the house—had six beds for the six of us and lively games were played into the night. Going to pee at night was a nightmare because the way to the loo was through the rooms haunted by Miss Perry. So whenever one child got up, the rest of us followed in a file lest we were forced to make the journey alone later. My cousin Pushpesh had created a Sanskrit mantra that he claimed would protect you from ghostly visitations if you recited it loudly. So the six of us would march in a procession, with Pushpesh leading us, torch in hand, and recite: *Pant putt mutt / Visarjan tarr-tarr sutt* (The Pant children are going to pee and as they pee tarr-tarr, please protect us!). We were poor, but as Diddi often reminded us later, like the Cratchits, we were happy and united in our poverty.

Perhaps it was the lack of money that was Diddi's motivation for taking up writing as a profession because she wrote furiously all the time. There is one story, among the earliest ones she published in *Dharmayug* in the fifties, called 'Lal Haveli' (The Red House) that has a haunting sense of regret for a life left behind. I think it has a subtext we all missed when we read it all those years ago.

~

Lal Haveli

A short story by Diddi (late 1950s):

Tahira glanced at her husband sleeping on the adjoining berth, sighed and turned over. Rehman Ali's paunch, swaddled under a blanket, was vibrating in consonance with the train's rhythm. Three hours to go. Tahira looked at the diamond-studded wristwatch on her slim wrist and cursed the damned thing. How slowly its hands moved! She hadn't been able to sleep a wink all night. She looked at her husband again and then at her daughter—both were dead to the world. Then a sudden attack of panic gripped her—whatever had she been thinking of when she agreed to her husband's proposed trip to India? She could have easily made some excuse and wriggled out. Time and a resolute blanking of memory had barely healed her wound— what had possessed her to scratch it open again?

At last the train steamed into the station and Tahira quickly covered her face with her silk burqa. Rehman Ali busied himself with getting their luggage sorted out, then helped his wife so tenderly out of the compartment that you would think she was a china doll that may break. Salma had jumped out first and a short, fat man huffing along the platform, cap in hand, had swept her up in his arms. Then he turned to Rehman Ali and embraced him tightly; their eyes were streaming with tears. So this is Mamu Bitte, the short uncle, Tahira realized, named *bitte* after his diminutive form. Mamu turned to Salma and kissed her: 'She is the replica of Ismat, Rehman,' he declared, caressing her face, 'those features again, the same face. Ismat's gone, so Allah sent us another Ismat.'

Tahira watched their reunion numbly: who would ever understand or see the turmoil that was raging in her heart? This railway station, the kaner tree—had nothing changed here in the last fifteen years?

'Come, my dear,' Mamu said, 'the car is waiting outside. It is a small district but this is Altaf's first posting. Inshallah, the next time we will go to a larger town.' It was for the wedding of Mamu's only son, Altaf, that Rehman Ali had come from Pakistan. Why on earth had destiny chosen to send Altaf as police inspector to this town, of all places in India, Tahira silently cursed.

When they reached home, the old grandmother went mad with joy. She hugged Rehman Ali and kissed him, then clasped Salma to her chest and forgot all about Tahira. 'Ya Khuda! What is this game You have played? You have sent my Ismat back to me again!' Both the daughters-in-law also echoed her, 'Truly, Ammijan, this is really Ismat Apa all over again. But won't you see the new bride's face? Here, give her this gold coin.'

Quickly, the old lady handed the coin to Tahira and lifted her burqa. 'Allah,' she exclaimed, 'this one is a beauty. Look at her— she is like a flame in a golden lamp.' Tahira blushed and bowed her head. This was her first visit to her in-laws in the last fifteen years and even now they had managed to get a visa to visit India for three days with great difficulty. But how would she last through these three long days?

'Go, child, go and rest in the room upstairs,' Mamu Bitte's wife suggested kindly. 'I'll send your tea there.' Tahira was taken upstairs, while Rehman Ali settled down with Mamu to catch up with the family's news. Salma was pulled into the grandmother's lap and the old lady ran her hands over her face and head repeating wonderingly, 'Ismat, my child, my dear child.'

In the privacy of her bedroom, Tahira flung off her burqa and opened the window. Then, she shrank back in horror— staring at her was the Lal Haveli. She quickly shut the window and stumbled to the bed. 'Oh God, why have you decided to torture me like this?' she sobbed. Who could she blame? She had known that the town that she was going to visit in India would open old wounds: how was her poor husband to know? The innocent Rehman Ali who worshipped Tahira and kept her in the lap of luxury—what did he know of her past ties? What could she say to him?

Tahira's story was of one of the many tragedies the Partition spawned. She was just sixteen at the time, and then a girl called Sudha. Sudha had accompanied her cousin to a wedding in her uncle's home in Multan when riots broke out between Hindus and Muslims. It was Rehman Ali who came like an angel to save her from the clutches of a horde of hoodlums who would surely have ripped her apart. They refused to let her go, saying that they were avenging what the Hindus had done to their women, but Rehman Ali managed to calm them down. A slim, dark youth, Rehman Ali took her under his wing and Sudha was saved as Tahira. Rehman's young wife had been killed by just such a mob in Delhi; he had managed to escape but what remained was a broken and saddened shadow of his former self.

Sudha held out against Rehman's proposal for a long time, but finally, on the condition that they would draw a veil of silence over her past, agreed to become his wife. Rehman Ali worshipped Tahira: if she had asked him to, he would have plucked the stars from the heavens and brought them to her. One smile from Tahira and Rehman Ali would be over the moon. A year later, she gave birth to a daughter and Rehman Ali forgot his past completely. He was convinced that Tahira had brought him good luck. Earlier, he had a small cloth shop in Karachi; today he was the owner of a departmental store, where attractive Anglo-Indian salesgirls sold imported stuff. The slim Rehman Ali filled out, acquired a paunch and his whole bearing changed. Even his speech had a trace of an American drawl now.

Decked with jewels, Tahira would toss restlessly on her huge carved bed. When March heralded the start of summer, Tahira was like a fish out of water, as she yearned for the fun-filled Holi of India. Where in Pakistan would she find the light-hearted banter that went with Holi? She remembered with pain one particular Holi and the pale pink muslin dupatta that Amma had trimmed with a golden border. Her young husband was reading some fat tome in his study and a lock of hair had fallen on his broad brow. A burnt-out cigarette dangled forgotten from one hand and as soon as he saw a flash of that pink dupatta, he bowed his head even deeper into the book—how shy he was with her! Sudha crept up silently behind him and rubbed colour on his cheeks, then darted back into the kitchen and began helping Amma with the gujiyas they used to make for the festival. Later, when her mother-in-law was not looking, she had poked a saucy pink tongue at him as he passed the kitchen door.

When she was leaving for Multan, how he had pleaded with her to not go: perhaps he had a premonition of what would happen if she went. He had come to see her off at the station—the same station she came to this morning—with its yellow kaner tree and its green railings. Sudha's face was covered with a veil then, yet as the train was steaming out of the station, she had peeked from behind it to see him standing on the platform—that was the last time she saw him.

But Sudha was dead and she was now Tahira. She went to the window once again and opened it with trembling hands to see her father-in-law's Lal Haveli once more. She could see the raat ki rani creeper on the terrace, and the third room upstairs where she had spent so many delicious nights in his arms. I wonder what he must be doing now, she thought; perhaps he also remarried and is playing with his children. Her eyes filled with tears as her heart considered these possibilities.

'Tahira, where are you?' she heard Rehman Ali call. She quickly wiped her face and started to wrestle with the bedding roll. One look at her tear-stained face and Rehman knelt near her, 'Now, now, biwi, what happened to you? Is your head hurting? Go on, go and lie down. How many times have I told you that you mustn't take on strenuous work, but who listens to me? There, lie down, and I'll tackle the unpacking.'

Tahira was made to lie down on a velvet mattress that had silken sheets: someone ran to fetch her a cool drink. Salma began pressing her head and Bari Ammi, the grandmother, declared it was the evil eye for sure! Najma was dispatched to fetch some red chillies and lime to throw into burning embers and avert the effects of this. Someone said it may be palpitations of the heart—the preserve of gooseberries would help.

After showering her with their loving advice, they all finally left. Rehman Ali, lying next to her, snored gently. Quietly, Tahira tiptoed to the window and stood gazing at the haveli. She was like a parched soul who had suddenly found a lake of clear water after an aeon—no matter how much water one drank, the thirst could not be quenched. A light was burning on the third floor. Dinner was always served rather late in that house and she used to carry a glass of milk to his room after it. Even after all these years, she remembered his every habit just as clearly as she remembered the arithmetic tables she had learnt as a child. Sudha, her conscience smote her, what were you thinking of when you agreed to marry someone else? Couldn't you have jumped into a well to save your honour? Had all the wells of Pakistan dried up? You may have given up your religion, but can you ever give up those traditions and rituals that were a part of you? You may have diverted the stream of your love but the chains that bind you to your past are unbroken. Every Holi, Diwali, Teej pierces your heart like a thorn. And why does Eid not fill you with the joy that others feel? There is your haveli, the home of your husband, go and fall at his feet and beg his forgiveness. Tahira stuffed her dupatta in her mouth to silence her sobs.

The bed groaned as Rehman Ali turned over in his sleep. Tahira tiptoed back to lie next to him.

The next day, the sound of shehnais floated up and the sound of rustling ghararas and dupattas scented with hina and motia filled the house. The police band was ready with the players smartly decked in their crisp uniforms and impressive turbans. All the women of the house would also go in the barat: young girls, with surma in their eyes and their rainbow-coloured wedding clothes, were falling over each other to get into the bus. A silken sheet had been drawn over the windows to shield them from male eyes and the older women, collecting their paandaans took a more leisurely attitude to the boarding. Covered in a black burqa, Tahira hung uncertainly on the fringes of this merry crowd. It was just such an evening, she recalled, when she had come to the Lal Haveli as a bride, covered in a red chunari. And here she was today, shrouded in a black burqa, aware that its blackness had snuffed out her old life completely.

'Did someone send a message to Vakil Sahib's house?' Bari Ammi called out and Tahira's heart froze.

'Yes, Ammi,' Mamujaan replied. 'He is not well and asked to be excused.'

'Such a decent man,' Ammi went on, as she opened a small box and stuffed a paan in her mouth. 'His father is the town's leading lawyer but he has no wife or child. I believe he lost his wife in the riots, so he decided to never marry again.'

It was a grand wedding and they returned with a doll-like bride. That evening everyone decided to go to see a film: the bride and groom, Bari Ammi, the girls and even the maids decked up for the outing. All except Tahira, who had a migraine—she felt she just did not have the energy to see some silly romantic rubbish. All she wanted was a darkened room and peace. She wanted to spend her last day in India all by herself.

The whole party left. Tahira got up, switched on the lights and stood in front of the mirror. Time and circumstances had not robbed her of any beauty—large eyes, flawless skin and a body made of marble. Who could say that she had a grown-up daughter? Tomorrow morning she would leave at four: could she not take just one look at the man who had taken a vow of celibacy after losing her? Her eyes shone like a naughty child's as she considered this.

She quickly flung a burqa over herself and came out of the room. With rapid steps, she ran to the haveli and stood outside it, sweating. She remembered the staircase at the rear that led straight to the small window in his room. Her feet seemed to have turned to lead and she felt she would suffocate with the excitement as she climbed to the room. She was no longer Tahira, but a sixteen-year-old called Sudha, who used to sneak past her vigilant mother-in-law to slyly visit her husband and colour him on Holi. Rehman Ali and his distinguished Sayyid ancestry receded from her mind. As she stood on the last step, she shut her eyes and muttered, 'O Baleshwar Mahadev, I will place this diamond ring at your feet if you allow me to see him without his knowing I am there watching him.' How could Lord Baleshwar not have granted her wish—after all, it was so long since he had heard his favourite devotee's voice! With tears almost blinding her, Sudha saw him. A grave man now, the love of her life was clad in a sparkling white pyjama and muslin kurta, looking just as he used to all those years ago. On his table was a picture of herself that her brother had once taken.

'Run now, Tahira, run!' it seemed to Sudha as if Lord Baleshwar himself was commanding her. She snapped out of her trance and Sudha became Tahira once again. She gazed at him one last time and, silently bidding him goodbye, ran to the small temple of Baleshwar Mahadev. How many boons she had sought here: today she would ask one last favour of him. Spreading her dupatta before his idol, she prayed, 'Keep him happy, Bholenath. May he never be hurt.' Then, she left her diamond ring at his feet and ran back.

Rehman Ali took one look at her pale face and immediately felt her pulse. 'No fever, I hope? Where is your ring, my dear?' He had given it to her on their wedding anniversary not long ago.

'I think I dropped it somewhere,' she replied wanly.

'Don't worry, love,' Rehman Ali kissed her fingers tenderly. 'As long as these fingers are mine, I'll cover them in diamonds. I'll order one from Teheran on our return.'

Tahira was gazing over his bent head at the Lal Haveli. Darkness was descending over it and the light in the third window was switched off. Tahira got up and shut the window.

Lal Haveli sank into darkness.

6

Binu

I was almost twelve before I discovered that Binu was not our 'real' sister. I must have been singularly foolish to never reflect on the fact that there was a striking lack of resemblance between us sisters. Minu and I shared the same colouring and features while Binu was entirely different: she had curly hair where ours was straight. Her eyes were larger, her skin darker and she was thin, whereas both Minu and I were plump. One of the first questions that most outsiders asked was why Binu looked so different from Minu and me. Diddi, however, was so good at deflecting these queries that both my brother and I were completely oblivious of the fact that Binu and we had different mothers.

When they were small, Diddi dressed Binu and Minu as twins and tried as hard as she could to make them look alike. I once asked Diddi who had given us our nicknames. Binu, she said. Binu insisted I call Minu 'Minu' because she was called Binu and you were called 'Mau' by her. (Apart from my father, no one else called me by that name, and Binu is still the only one who calls me 'Mau'.) But who named Binu 'Binu' I persisted. Oh Binu came to me as Binu, Diddi smiled. And I went away satisfied that—like some self-realized saint—Binu was, and will always be, Binu.

I remember very clearly how I learnt the truth about Binu. I was fond of wandering over to the office section of Priory Lodge to tap on a typewriter or just scribble with some pencils and paper. The clerks were more than happy to take time off and I chatted for hours with them about their families. 'So where is your stepsister?' one asked me one day. 'Stepsister? Who do you mean?' I countered. 'Oh, you mean you don't know?' he said and then shut up as someone else probably kicked him under the table. 'My God, what a woman your mother must be!' he muttered to himself.

I raced up the stairs and burst into my mother's room. Diddi was, as usual, writing. 'Di!' I blurted out, 'Is it true that we have a stepsister?' She looked up from the page in front of her. 'Who said that to you?' I named the clerk downstairs in Babu's office. 'How many times have I told you not to go to the office?' she said angrily. 'Babu will be furious if he hears you went there. Go outside and play or read a book or something,' she said.

But the cat was out of the bag. Later, of course, there were other people who dropped bricks about this subject and I came to accept that Binu was our half-sister. Strangely, this made all of us even fonder of her and I remember vowing that I would never hurt her by ever saying a cruel word. Minu and I, on the other hand, fought all the time. But Binu was the one person whom none of us ever had a problem with: when I look back, I realize she was a sort of surrogate mother to Micky and me and made up for Diddi's absent-minded mothering by being loving and kind.

As we grew older and she accepted that we had found out her secret, Diddi would occasionally let slip a word or two about Binu's mother. How they were friends before she was married to Babu. How when she and Jayanti came back from Santiniketan, Ganga borrowed a blouse of Diddi's to copy its pattern. Yet nothing deeper or more painful ever escaped her lips. No confidences on what she felt when she was married to a man who had lost his wife a bare year ago, nothing about bringing Binu into her life or the first few days. Nothing.

After Diddi's death, one day as Binu and I were sorting out her books, papers and photographs, I decided to ask Binu about something that had troubled me for some time. Isn't it strange, I remarked to Binu, that there is no picture of your mother among Diddi's things? Wait, said Binu mysteriously, I have something to show you. She took out an old tin box from her cupboard and out came a handful of pictures of Ganga and my father. Diddi gave this to me along with my mother's jewellery when I got married, she told me. And we pored over the studio portrait of Babu and Ganga taken shortly after they were married.

I cannot tell you what it was like to see my father standing next to a wife who was not Diddi. The photograph blurred before me and then came back into focus again. I looked carefully at the face of the woman who had been an unspoken ghost in our lives for a lifetime. No one spoke of her and no one dared to ask what she was like. After I got married, I heard of her from my mother-in-law, who had been friends with her in their girlhood. She was a spirited young thing, I was told, and your father and she faced such opposition from his family before they were married! She loved eating red chillies and sipping hot tea with them. The day before she got married, she ate so many raw apricots that she got the runs and fainted halfway through the wedding. Your father had to carry her home...

I looked critically at the picture again. She died when she was not even twenty-five years old, my mind kept repeating, not even twenty-five. She was beautiful in the wistful and innocent way unique to all those who die young. Ganga was dark, she had deep pools of sadness for eyes and she was dainty and small.

If she had lived on, would she have retained that delicate beauty or would she have bloated into a fat, ungainly shrew? Who knows, but what I came to realize was that this is the picture of Ganga that Babu must have frozen in his heart. 'Forever will he love and she be fair…' I remembered Keats as I looked away from her face to my father's, and saw the love and pride in his eyes. His brooding silences and inexplicable black moods began to acquire a shape in my mind now.

It was at that moment, and for the first time, that I began to understand what it must have meant for Diddi to marry a man who still grieved for his first wife and what it must have meant to Diddi to remain second best all her life. Her eagerness to get Babu's approval, a kind word, a compliment—all of this had a history that I was beginning to see for the first time.

At fifty-two, I was able to understand more than I could take at twelve. At twelve, when I first realized that Binu had lost her mother when she was one or so, my sympathies were for her. Now, they swung in the direction of a woman who was young, talented and a free spirit, popular among her friends and admired for her mind and voice at Santiniketan, who had to forget all she was the day she became my father's second wife. In 'Lal Haveli', Tahira is forced to forget her past and adopt a new life; it was a pain that Diddi had known too.

Why did you never put a picture of your mother in your home after you got married, I asked Binu. I just never could: I never knew her, Binu said simply. Diddi was the only mother I knew and I could never get myself to put my mother's picture as long as Diddi was alive or ever find the courage to ask Diddi or anyone else what my mother was like. I had decided very long ago to respect the silence that she left in our lives. And now that Diddi is gone, this is just a picture, she said, and put the photos back in the box.

And yet, Diddi did write of Ganga and my father. In a poignant short story, published in the sixties, called 'Lati', Diddi told her readers the truth about the love of Babu's life.

~

Lati

A short story by Diddi (late 1960s):

The sharp rays of the sun pierced the tall deodars stooping over the roof of Gethiya Sanatorium and bounced off its shining windowpanes. The patients inside opened their eyes, blinking at the brightness of the morning sun and, for a brief while, their wan faces lit up.

Today, when tuberculosis is considered almost as harmless as a bad bout of the flu, it is difficult to describe how once the mere mention of its name sent shivers down your spine. In those pre-penicillin days, the sanatorium at Gethiya was in greater demand than the even more famous Bhowali Sanatorium. Its cluster of cheery red roofs nestled in the hills above Kathgodam looked like a bright bouquet buried among the deodars.

Captain Joshi had paid double the normal fee for Bungalow Number Three to personally nurse his young wife, Bano. He placed an armchair next to her lounger in the veranda and would spend the whole day at her bedside, filling her temperature chart, or carefully measuring out her medicines before handing them tenderly to her. Their daily romantic tableau was a source of great pleasure to the patients in the neighbouring cottages, who watched these lovebirds with envy and indulgence. There seemed no end to the man's patience: he'd even brush his wife's hair! And occasionally, when he sang Pahari folksongs to her, his voice reminded them of the sound of the deep cowbells they'd heard in their childhood. 'Don't stop, captain,' they cheered him on. 'Come on, give us another song.' And the captain obliged them after a long, loving look at his wife.

Her illness had given Bano's face a pleasing pallor and made her large eyes enormous. Their serene gaze constantly followed her husband. This was their honeymoon really, for although they had been married for two years, this was the first time there were no in-laws to keep them apart, no cruel barbs and no errands for Bano to run. It was as if someone had miraculously opened the door of her cage but, sadly, her weak wings no longer had the strength to fly. Her slender wrist almost disappeared in the robust clasp of her husband and the bangles she wore on them now slid up to her elbows.

The director of the Gethiya Sanatorium was a Swiss doctor. One day he sent for the captain. 'You are a young man, captain,' he said, 'and I want to warn you that this disease thrives on young blood. I notice you take no precautions to save yourself from getting infected. But I'd like you to remember, young man, that no amount of love can defeat this disease.'

The captain flushed with embarrassment. His parents had already written countless letters, pleading with him to return home. 'I don't have any other son,' his mother had written, 'so why are you deliberately courting death?' Yet the captain refused to leave his wife's bedside. He kissed her hair, her silky lashes and stayed on in defiance of all advice. Once in a while, he would walk across to the Private Ward next door and visit the fat and jolly wife of a rich contractor, Guman Singh, affectionately called Bhabhi by everyone.

Bhabhi was the one ray of sunshine in an atmosphere heavy with intimations of mortality. Her round, fair face was always smiling, and everyone wondered how TB had managed to make a dent in the well-fortified walls of her frame. Once in a while, especially when she was in pain, she would let loose a hail of curses against the world. Often the target was her father-in-law: 'The old man owns half of Kumaon but does he care if his daughter-in-law is going to die? No sir!' she would declare to the delight of her audience. 'Lift the tail of any male in my family, and you'll discover a cunt not balls!'

'Bravo! That one was straight out of *Punch* magazine,' the captain applauded. 'You've made my day, Bhabhi,' he told her. Encouraged by his response, she took off, 'And then there is my husband, the son of a bitch. I'm sure he must be lying drunk in the arms of some trashy white tart. D'you know that it's been two months since the bastard came here? May his bones rot—see if I mourn him when he dies!'

'Oh come on, Bhabhi,' the captain ribbed her, 'why curse your own husband?' She hooted with laughter and her eyes filled up as she looked at him with love. 'Hats off to you, son, for the way you care for your wife. When I see you with her, I swear my breasts fill up with milk... And look at my bastard! I tell you I'll stuff his whiskers in his mouth if he comes anywhere near me!'

The captain doubled up with laughter and he ran to share this latest gem with his Bano.

Then one day, the captain heard an incessant, hacking cough from the direction of Bhabhi's cottage. He ran across to see her lying in a pool of blood. Her vast body was lying inert and her face was deathly pale. So Bhabhi had left before she could stuff her husband's whiskers in his mouth. For a few days, a pall of gloom descended over the captain's life and Bano's large sad eyes grew larger with fear. If such a healthy, happy woman could go like a puff of smoke, what hope was there for her? She was so frail that even a whiff of a breeze could blow her away like a fluffy ball of cotton. Bhabhi's death had brought them a message they had ignored for so long—that there was some respite, never a reprieve, from death. But it also made them determined to extract what they could from these last days of happiness—Bano became like a spoilt child, demanding attention all the time, and the captain played along with her, pandering to her every ridiculous whim. He took her to sit in the moonlit garden, swaddling her in his army greatcoat, and cuddled her close to his warm body. For a long time, they gazed at the stars under the whispering deodars, lost in their own thoughts.

Exactly three days after they got married, he had left Bano to go to Basra. Overwhelmed by his huge physique and bushy moustache, Bano ran away shyly each time he came near her. Her dainty hennaed hands covered her face and it was with great difficulty that he had managed to get her to tell him her name. With his uncle sleeping in the next room, all conversation between them had to be conducted in furtive whispers.

'What is you name?' he whispered, tilting her pointed chin in his hands.

'Bano,' she fluttered through downcast eyes.

'Sounds like a Muslim name to me,' he joked.

'That's what everyone says,' her large eyes filled up. 'It's not my fault!'

'I was just joking! It's beautiful and such a delightful change from the usual run of Pahari names—Saruli, Paruli, Rama, Khashti… How old are you, Bano?'

'This summer I'll be sixteen,' she said proudly as if she had reached a huge age. The captain shook his head at her innocence as he gathered her to his breast. What a child she was! When his father and uncle had decided on Bano, he had been livid. How could they think of marrying him, a man about town, to a girl

111

fresh out of school? But now, he had lost his heart completely to this little schoolgirl.

Three days later it was time for him to go to Basra. When he went to say goodbye to her, Bano was sitting in a corner, cutting suparis. Her eyelashes were wet and the moment she heard her husband's footfall, she buried her head in her knees. He bent and quickly kissed the top of her head and his throat contracted as he strode out.

Leaving a three-day-old bride was a harder prospect than facing the cannon fire of the enemy lines. For two years, he was in Basra and then in Burma. All his friends succumbed to loneliness and the charms of the local Burmese beauties but not the captain. Yet when he returned home two years later, he found everything had changed. Bano had spent those years listening to the barbs directed at her by seven sisters-in-law, washed mounds of their children's clothes, knitted dozens of socks for the captain's uncles and her father-in-law, and ground mountains of urad dal to make baris and mungauris that she had to dry on the tin roofs of the house. She had no idea where the captain was: one day they would tell her he was lost in some battle, another that he would never return. With this came the curses on her head for bringing such bad luck to their home that they had lost their only son. Finally, TB hunted her down and she was packed off to a sanatorium. To the great disappointment of his family, the captain rushed off the very next day after he returned from war to see Bano at the sanatorium.

When he saw her lying in the sanatorium bed, his heart skipped a beat. In two years, it seemed to him, she had regressed further into girlhood and looked like a child lying there. Her eyes registered her disbelief and then the tears started to flow. There was no need for words—her tears had laid bare all her

112

suffering. That is when they both realized that this was their only chance of time together and it was running out fast.

The captain and Bano mourned Bhabhi's death for about three days and were back on their honeymoon on the fourth. Bano asked him to take out her trunk of saris and get them ironed. Then they played patience for a long while but by the evening, Bano started to wilt. She had been running to the toilet all afternoon and when the runs come to a TB patient, death cannot be far behind. In those days, the sanatorium heartlessly turned out a dying patient to save the rest of the inmates from getting affected by a death on the premises, for death was cruelly debarred from entering the sanatorium gates. As he made his evening rounds, the doctor called the captain outside and handed him a notice: 'You will have to take her home tomorrow. I give her two-three days,' he said. 'I doubt she will last longer in her condition.'

The captain's face went white. How could he possibly take her home now and erase these three months of bliss to return to the misery of his parents' home? He knew of a place near a tea shop at Bhowali where he could take her to die. The owner always understood the predicament of those who had been sent a passport to another world and kept some rooms open for them.

'Let's leave the sanatorium, Bano,' he announced cheerily to her that night. 'We'll leave tomorrow. I'm fed up with the place— aren't you?' Bano blanched: she was no fool and understood immediately what the doctor had said to her husband a while ago. She had been given the notice to leave Gethiya.

That night, he nuzzled her neck on the pillow with his face, 'Bano, my Banni, Bannoo!' he whispered to cheer her. Finally, when she dropped off, he lay down on his bed and slept.

The next morning he awoke to find Bano missing. At first he thought she must have dragged herself to the loo. Often she would do that rather than ask for help but when she did not come out for a long time, he ran to bang on the door. Bano was nowhere to be found. He ran all over the sanatorium but no one had seen her. Soon the room filled up with anxious doctors, nurses and the security staff. Nothing like this had ever happened at the sanatorium.

The next day they found her sari at Rathighat and everyone deduced that Bano had decided to meet death before it could come and drag her away. There was no doubt that she had committed suicide. Maddened with grief, the captain hugged her sari and dredged the river but Bano was gone.

His youth stretched ahead of him like a long winter's night: how long could he stay alone? Within a year, his family married him off again and this time his father and uncle made sure that the girl was healthy. The captain's new wife was a tall and strapping girl, and had a master's degree to boot. Her father was a major general and when he flashed his row of medals at the wedding, the poor captain knew he was outshone by far. Prabha, that was her name, was an only and spoilt child used to having her way. Her unending commands and high expectations made the captain forget how to crack jokes or even laugh.

Over the next four years, Prabha gave him two sons and a daughter and then turned her attention to saving money. After sixteen years, when Prabha decided they had saved enough, she agreed to visit the hills for the first time and they decided to go to Nainital for a holiday. The captain now had a neat little paunch and his face, though still good-natured and decorated with a bristling moustache, lacked the freshness of his youth. His sons had got their army commissions and the daughter was studying at Miranda House in Delhi.

As they drove up from Kathgodam, old memories came crowding into his mind at each turn the car took. And when they passed Gethiya, the captain lapsed into a moody silence.

Prabha had booked them in the Grand Hotel in Nainital and after unpacking, she said, 'Come on, darling, let's go for a drive. I want to see Bhowali.' She ordered a picnic hamper of sandwiches and roast chicken and they both drove off. Just short of Bhowali, Prabha, glowing in her Chanderi sari and sleeveless blouse, patted him with a plump hand. 'Stop! Let's stop at that darling little tea shop and have a Pahari-style glass of tea, please!'

'And what about a major's dignity?' he asked.

'Oh, to hell with it,' she laughed and got off, balancing herself carefully on her pencil heels.

The tea shop had a solitary wooden bench and the tin roof was grimy with years of woodsmoke. The poor owner was overwhelmed at this sudden invasion and tried to fiddle with the kettle boiling on his stove.

'Two hot glasses of tea, Pradhan-jyu,' the major said to him in Pahari to put him at ease. The man's jaw dropped open at someone like the major speaking the local patois. Had they lost their way? Why on earth would a dazzling couple like them visit his humble dhaba, he wondered.

He was still brewing the tea when they heard 'Alakh, Alakh' and a band of Vaishnavi sadhvis descended. 'Oh ho, guru,' said the leader in a deep contralto. 'Thought we'd drop by at your shop and give my flock a glass of tea made by a Brahmin's hands.'

'Good, good,' the shopkeeper smiled. 'Have you brought Lati as well?'

'Where else would she go, poor thing?' replied the head. And the major and Prabha turned their heads to see who they referred to.

She stood like an apsara among this band of old, withered women and revealed pearly teeth as she smiled in acknowledgement. The major went numb: it was as if Bano

115

had been miraculously cured and was standing before him. Her cheeks were pink with health and her face looked even more beautiful and innocent now that she could not speak any more.

'Poor thing, is she dumb?' Prabha asked the head Vaishnavi. 'My god! What a beauty!' she turned to her husband for corroboration.

'Yes, madam,' piped in the shopkeeper. 'She has no tongue.' The major felt as if a huge weight had suddenly been lifted from his chest.

'What is her name?' Prabha couldn't take her eyes off the vision.

'God knows, memsahib,' the head Vaishnavi said. 'All that went a long time ago. Our guru maharaj found her floating in the river one day. Her tongue had been bitten off. Must have been married because she was wearing a mangalsutra but who knows who her husband was or where he went. Our guruji gave a mantra to cure her of the terrible TB she had. She used to vomit buckets of blood when we found her but after guruji took her under his wing, she was completely cured. Show them your tongue, Lati,' she commanded.

The beauty just smiled but refused to show her tongue.

'Can't follow anything, the stupid cow,' the Vaishnavi explained helpfully. 'All she does is eat and crap. She's lost it, I think, doesn't follow my orders at all.'

'Oh my God!' Prabha said. 'You mean she's even forgotten her husband?'

'Who knows?' replied the Vaishnavi philosophically. 'The past is the past. She doesn't remember anything. Just smiles all the time, the cow. Who does she have now but God to look after her?' Then she turned her attention to the shopkeeper. 'So how much do I owe you, guru?'

She paid up and with a loud 'Alakh!' her band followed her

out of the shop. Lati sat on, and the major could not take his eyes off her. Dr Dalal and Dr Kakkar had failed to cure her—could it be true that she was cured by a guruji and that this was his Bano?

'Get up!' the head Vaishnavi gave Lati a jab with her toe. Lati turned once to flash a smile at the major and then followed her leader down the hill.

If he nuzzled her neck with his face and said, 'My Bano, Banni, Bannu!' would it unlock her frozen memory, he wondered as he watched her walk away. But how could that be possible? He had taken another path, climbed another mountain. Moreover, he said to himself, has anyone ever gained anything from glancing over his shoulder to pick up the pieces of the past? He had two grown sons now, and a daughter. And what of his wife, Prabha, with her plans for their future? What would he say to them if he brought a dumb beauty into their lives?

'Come, darling,' Prabha said. 'Let's have lunch in Garampani.' The major got up slowly, like a man who has aged suddenly. He was numb and empty.

His Bano was dead. And now God looked after Lati.

He followed his wife dutifully to the car.

7

Jayanti Jerja

My aunt Jayanti—brilliant and kinky in equal measure—and Diddi were kindred souls. In the years that we were at Priory Lodge, we frequently visited Mukteswar, where Jayanti Jerja (this is what we called her, a title that means older mother in Kumaoni) and her doctor husband lived. Today, Mukteswar is merely an hour's drive from Nainital but in the sixties, you had to spend almost three hours in a jolting bus, and fight the nauseating diesel fumes it belched as it climbed the steep bends and twists. It was a journey that left us puking and dizzy when we disembarked. Jerja could never get herself to brave this journey and so, although her sons studied in Nainital, she rarely came to visit us. And when she did, she came in a *dandi*, borne on the shoulders of Nepali coolies—an expedition that took almost two days.

This curious caravan (with two or three servants and several pieces of baggage, carried by still more coolies) was a visit we really looked forward to. Jayanti Jerja would unpack her bright parcels and huge tiffin carriers of food almost as soon as she got off. Out would come home-made Gujarati pickles and savouries, delicious milk sweets prepared in her kitchen from the rich, creamy milk of her hybrid cows and fresh fruit and preserves made from her garden produce. Every night, we would snuggle close to her bed while she told us macabre ghost stories and sang songs in Gujarati and Bengali to illustrate them. What stories they were—tales of ghostly apparitions, sadhus who could foresee dire events, magical tortoises, and stars that came at night to whisper secrets into her ears alone. Of course, we believed her implicitly. She convinced my little brother Micky, who she loved above us all, that he was born after she had made a special prayer for him at the Shiva temple of Mukteswar Mahadev and jumped through a hole in a rocky outcrop at the far end of the town. This is why he was named Muktesh, she said. According to another magical tale, she and he were two divine storks in their earlier life. Reunited in this birth as human beings, she called him 'Bagula' (Mr Stork) and made him call her 'Baguli' (Mrs Stork), a name that he continued to call her by until she died. In short, Jerja was a one-woman entertainment industry: she could conjure spirits from the vasty deep and make you believe in them.

The minute she stepped into Priory Lodge, the strict rules of our house were magically relaxed. Among the most hated of Babu's commandments were no reading novels in the forenoon, no eating between meals, no standing on a bed or running up a staircase, no reading comics or romantic, mushy pulp fiction, no laughing loudly, no listening to film music, no playing cards and gitti... Jerja's children broke all the rules that we were subjected to: they ate in bed and never brushed their teeth before sleeping; they seldom had a bath; they did not make their beds or fold their clothes and—to our great envy—they got away with all these violations. When Jerja came to Priory Lodge, even Babu, who seldom stepped into the children's room, found his way there to listen to her fascinating tales. Mealtimes were disrupted and, for once, Babu allowed someone else's writ to run his house. Jerja's servants were given a kitchen downstairs where they cooked for themselves and their chatter filtered up to our rooms, yet Babu never frowned at this just as he no longer frowned if we laughed loudly or banged doors. Diddi and Jerja would lie on adjoining beds every afternoon, with the maids pressing their feet, as they exchanged stories and confidences. To prevent any eavesdroppers from listening in, they switched easily into Gujarati or Bengali and this was certainly my first lesson in the two languages.

Jerja was the archetypal Earth Mother. She loved bright colours and wore a large bindi on her forehead and vermilion in the parting of her hair. Her dainty feet were covered with toerings and tinkling anklets while glass bangles covered her arms. Her Mukteswar bedroom had a glass case with colourful glass bangles and she would change them each day to match her clothes. She ordered by post any hair oil or perfume that caught her fancy and had all manner of herbal concoctions on her bedside table. Many of these she had created herself and they had hilarious names and histories. One that caused much merriment among us was christened 'Krishna mastana tel' and smelt of jasmine. It was a massage oil she had created to madden the senses of her husband, Krishna. Jerja had small hands and feet but was deep-bosomed and exuded a fecundity that was warm and perfumed. She did everything with a joyous abandon—I cannot think of any other phrase that could better describe her free and open nature. Her love for her family and the complete lack of any self-consciousness in displaying her love for her husband is what I remember most, for it was a quality I missed in my parents' relationship. I do not ever remember Babu touching Diddi in our presence, whereas Jerja and her husband called each other 'dear' and 'darling' freely. At night, she would slip into his bed, without caring whether the child sleeping with her that night (she always had one snuggled next to her, like a hot water bottle) was awake and watching.

Her Mukteswar house was a child's paradise: a vast library that had hundreds of books, including many that she had rescued from termites and silverfish in Kasoon. The walls of her sitting room were covered with family portraits that had the whole Kasoon clan framed and preserved. Everything was painted a dark green and Jerja's taste in decor ran into the baroque and bizarre. There were clocks and paintings my uncle had bought from departing Englishmen who sold their apple orchards in Kumaon after 1947, when many of them returned to their own country. These sat uncomfortably with the baubles that Jerja collected from everywhere: a shell from Puri, a doll from Bhopal, a rug from a passing Tibetan vendor, huge spring beds that we bounced on, and curtains with frills. Her house also had several cats and when you were not tumbling over them, you ran into a servant. It was a mini-Kasoon, for several old servants from Ama's home had migrated to Mukteswar and were now part of Jayanti Jerja's colourful household. Among them was Khyali, Lohaniji's son, who had blue eyes and spoke in English to us. Khyali sat on the front veranda, trimming the betel leaves that arrived by post every week from Banaras for my uncle.

Kishan Bhinju, Jerja's husband, was a fastidious sahib but soon, under the influence of Jerja's crazy lifestyle, he went native. He gave up his tweeds and flannels and, after his retirement, wore only saffron-coloured clothes to indicate his retreat from worldly desires. However, Jerja managed to infiltrate even this retreat and had exotic chiffon kurtas made for him and teemed them up with khadi pyjamas or trousers. She, of course, always dressed in the brightest saris with the loudest prints. Their bedroom always smelt of musk and saffron because of the scented tobacco that my uncle was fond of chewing.

Every summer, the Mukteswar house would fill up with guests—some, like us, were family, others were old friends from Santiniketan and some were just friends of friends. Jayanti Jerja was in her element then: cooking, talking and matchmaking. Someone had gifted Pushpesh and Muktesh a tape recorder—a new gadget for us in the sixties—and Pushpesh and my sister Mrinal wrote plays that were enacted by all the children gathered there and played to the family after dinner. The sunny front veranda had a swing (in memory of their Gujarat childhood) and we fought with each other for the privilege to swing and read on it. Like Ama, Jerja seldom went anywhere but seemed to know of all the town's gossip and took an active role in other people's intimate family problems. She encouraged children to gossip—to our great delight—for we all loved reporting to her. Over the dinner table at night, she would proceed to tell the family of all that she had garnered from her army of reporters: the compounder at the hospital was having an affair with the staff nurse's daughter. The headman of a neighbouring village had reported how they had cut off the balls of a young boy who had dared to sleep with a girl of another caste... It was better than reading the morning newspaper and bred in all of us a great taste for the sensational and bizarre.

Mukteswar's modest government-run primary school was little better than a village school. So Jerja gave her children lessons at home until they were ready to enter the university. This is when Pushpesh and Muktesh came to stay with us in Nainital. Pushpesh was just sixteen and Muktesh a year older. By the time he was twenty-one, Pushpesh had finished his Ph.D. and left to teach at the prestigious Jawaharlal Nehru University in Delhi. Unlike our house, where Diddi and Babu kept a stern watch on our school performance, Jerja's children never felt intimidated by exams simply because they never went to school. Pushpesh and Minu were phenomenal readers and thanks to Diddi and Jerja's unorthodox teaching styles were fluent in Sanskrit as well as English. I hero-worshipped them both and aped their reading habits and speed. Thus by the time I was twelve or so, I had read whatever books the house had—an eclectic mix of adult books and romances ranging from Aldous Huxley to Pearl Buck. Of course, I did not understand most of them but it gave me a great sense of power over my schoolmates who were still reading Enid Blyton and Georgette Heyer.

After they left Mukteswar, Jerja and her family moved to Bhowali, where they lived in a cottage called The Hermitage. Soon this began to resemble the Mukteswar house and my children insisted on a mandatory stop there on our way to Almora each summer. My cousin Muktesh, who never worked all his life and was never asked any uncomfortable questions regarding this, was generally to be found reading in a bed and received visitors in a supine state. Jerja would take the children on a conducted tour of the house and stop every now and then to point out a special feature and to show them her books and treasures. Then she would tell them about all the spirits who had visited her recently. Finally, we were given pumpkins and fruit from her garden to take to various people in Almora as gifts. Why she imagined pumpkins would be welcome as a gift we never asked and tried to make place for them in the car. One year when we reached her Bhowali cottage, she was standing waist-deep in a drum, washing a vast cotton durrie by treading on it. She looked as happy as if she was pressing juice from grapes in a vineyard and waved cheerily to us as we climbed the hill to her cottage. She seemed to be having such fun that my children promptly took off their shoes and socks and took turns jumping in and out of the drum. Her magic was

123

undimmed by age and she could still charm the parrots off a tree.

~

A River That Lost Its Way in Sand

Diddi's article on Jerja, written in the early 1990s, is my personal favourite among all the obituaries that Diddi wrote. It still brings tears to my eyes when I see the Jerja we all loved emerge from Diddi's pen.

The hot summer has melted into an unbearably humid rainy season—whatever happened to the refreshing coolness of the month of Asadh, I wonder, mopping my brow. Then, out of the shimmering heat, a beloved face floats out and I can hear her voice reading Kalidasa's immortal lines from *Meghdoot* to me: *Dhrumjyoti salilmara...*

Jayanti was the second of us seven sisters. Early this year, news of her terminal illness reached me in Lucknow and I rushed to Delhi to her bedside. What I saw shocked me: gone was the glowing olive colour of her skin and her musical voice was now a whispered croak. She held out her thin arms to embrace me and started to weep. I had never ever seen her cry and we both realized that this was probably a prelude to a final separation. As I held her trembling body, I felt unable to bring myself to say anything at all. We both knew it was too late for all that.

She drew back, passed a loving hand over my head and said sheepishly, 'I don't know what happens to me nowadays, the waterworks just don't stop. How are you?' One claw-like hand clasped mine and the other trailed like a withered creeper across the bed. Her arms had become so thin that the bangles slithered up to her shoulder. Her eyes, clouded with cataracts, were straining to focus on my face and I was almost glad that she could not see it. Nor could I answer her loving question. With a long sigh, she closed her eyes, folded her arms over her chest, closed her eyes and withdrew to some inner world.

Earlier, when she did that Jayanti meditated, and her face would turn luminous with peace. It was her secret way of communing with her inner self and her mind. And what a mind! The Banaras Hindu University once conferred the degree of Sahitya Mahishini on her. From her childhood, she had lived with our grandfather, an awesome scholar of Sanskrit, and her skill at languages was legendary. Gujarati, Bengali, Marathi, Urdu, Hindi, English, Sanskrit, Pali, Prakrit—she was fluent in all of these. At Santiniketan, she studied Chinese under Professor Ta'an but Sanskrit was her mother tongue. When she wrote, it was like a piece of jewellery: sparkling and pure. So when in her old age, her hand started to tremble and her half-blind eyes no longer obeyed her, it made me weep to read her scrawl. Reading was her life and when her eyes failed her, she died a little each day.

For some reason, she never pursued her skill at storytelling. Had she done so, I am convinced she would have been one of the finest writers of her generation. *Chand* and *Hans* had published her early writing and one of her stories was included in the academic syllabus of the Viswa Bharati University but then, for some inexplicable reason, she stopped writing. Her collection of letters alone was fit for a museum's collection. Premchand, Jainendra, Rabindranath Tagore, Nandlal Bose, Alice Boner, Acharya Kriplani, Madan Mohan Malviya, Balraj Sahni—Jayanti used to correspond with all of them. How I wish I had asked her for these letters before she died. I cannot remember how many letters Acharya Hajari Prasad Dwivedi had written to her. Gurudev painted a portrait with colours she herself had collected from wild plants, after consulting the Vanaushadhi Parva of the Amar Kosh.

Last year, the Bengali magazine *Desh* published a letter by Tagore where he mentions how his beloved student Jayanti had collected haridra, khadir, palash and burunsh to extract vegetable colours for his paintings. I sent her a cutting. When I met her a few months later, I asked, 'Did you read that article?' 'I can't find it,' she replied. 'I'd put it under my pillow and it seems to have disappeared. What did it say?' she asked me disarmingly.

I shook my head in exasperation. Her 'pillow bank' was a notorious Bermuda Triangle where things mysteriously vanished. You could find everything from dried fruits to old photographs to forbidden sweets (she was diabetic). Surrounded by such distractions, what could that poor article have done but disappear?

Jayanti's tragedy was that she never gave her genius the honour it deserved. That honour was given it by Gurudev and the gurus of our Ashram. Hajari Prasad Dwivedi used to say, 'One day, Jayanti will inherit my pen.' Gurudev had nicknamed her Bharat Mata, or Mother India. With her thick khaddar saris, hitched inches above her ankles, her abstract gaze and remote expression, she evoked laughter from some and envy from others. Her closeness to Gurudev was for all to see—he showered her with such love and attention that many declared Jayanti had become proud.

This was not true: pride and Jayanti could never be synonymous. Although, God knows, she had every reason to be arrogant. She was beautiful, accomplished and respected in the Ashram. Her beauty—which shone through the hideous homespun saris she wore—was incandescent. This was evident from the proposals that my mother began to receive for her when Jayanti passed her Intermediate exam. But Jayanti had announced long ago that she would never marry. My mother used to coax her saying, 'Look Jayanti, proposals such as these don't come every day—where will you find such boys and such families? You are eighteen—your elder sister was a mother at fourteen. This boy has gone abroad to take his ICS exam…' But Jayanti was adamant: she would never marry.

Among her suitors was a dandy, nicknamed 'Lord', who found many excuses those days to pass our house. I remember how livid Jayanti was when she saw him—resplendent in a tweed jacket, cigar in hand—eyeing her from the road outside our house. 'Listen,' she told me. 'I'll give you five rupees—spit on his brilliantined hair and tell him, "My sister will never marry you."' I accepted the offer with alacrity—five rupees was a lot of money in the thirties. The next day, Lord came on his usual evening stroll and stopped outside our house—as he often did then—preparing to strike the appropriate pose for gazing at Jayanti. I had lovingly nursed a ball of spit in my mouth all evening for just this occasion. The missile went flying out of my mouth and landed neatly on his pomaded locks. 'Scram,' I yelled rudely. 'My sister has said she will never marry you.'

That was the last we ever saw of him but I still blush when I remember my uncouth behaviour. Years later, the poet Sumitranandan Pant wrote a story on Lord's proposal in a collection of stories called *Paanch Phool*.

Meanwhile, Jayanti was determined not to marry. She had by now passed her MA and was offered a wardenship at Santiniketan, where she also taught. Most of her time, however, was spent with Gurudev at Uttarayan and whenever he went to Mussoorie or Almora, Jayanti was his constant companion. When Mahatma Gandhi visited Santiniketan, Jayanti was chosen to receive him. A photograph taken by the famous photographer

Shambhu Saha shows Gandhiji getting out of his car, his hand on Jayanti's shoulder, Ba on one side and a loving Rabindranath looking on.

Last year, I asked her, 'Where is that picture? Or is that lost as well?'

'God knows who flicked it from my album,' she said ruefully.

'And that poem written for you by Gurudev from Darjeeling? Where is that?'

'Lost as well,' she said.

I used to get livid with her—what treasures she had managed to lose! Yet there was one she never let out of her sight—this was a portrait of her painted by Tagore with the colours she had mixed for him. Inscribed 'Jayanti ke Rabindranath' (To Jayanti from Rabindranath), it was always on her bedside table.

Come to think of it, Gurudev was not wrong when he named Jayanti Bharat Mata—she was a born social worker. I have lost count of how many students she taught and how many destitute girls she educated and married off. Her husband was a doctor (Yes, she did marry later. It was a fairly radical event for those days.) and they lived in an idyllic house in Mukteswar in the Kumaon hills. They had a garden full of flowers and fruit trees, dozens of helpers—Jaikishen, Bishandutt, Daulat, Salim—and two fat Australian hybrid cows. Virtually all of Mukteswar had free access to her dairy and there was no expectant mother who did not receive a pail of pure milk from Jayanti's dairy. She would make the most delicious rasgullas and sandesh and I can vouch that even Bhimnag and Bambajari in Calcutta never produced anything like her sweets. Married to a doctor, Jayanti naturally offered free treatment and medicines to everyone.

I remember a particularly gruesome incident. A grass cutter was attacked by a bear who clawed out his nose while the man was out in the jungle. However, his doughty wife packed the mauled nose in snow and husband and wife landed up at her house (I was spending a vacation with Jayanti then) at two in the morning. It was bitterly cold and a snowstorm was raging outside. Several tall deodars, unable to bear the weight of the snow on their branches, had snapped like matchsticks and keeled over. Power lines had collapsed and there was no light anywhere except for the deathly white glow of the snow around us. Only the truly mad would venture out on a night like that.

Naturally, we stepped out, and the half-frozen woman, holding up her fainting, noseless husband, fell at our feet. 'Help me, Dactrani-jyu,' she called out to Jayanti. 'Please save my man's life.' I took one look at the hideous, noseless lump of bleeding flesh in front of us and ran inside. Within minutes, there was blood all over the veranda, squirting in a steady stream from the hole in the man's face. Jayanti came inside to persuade my sleeping brother-in-law to take the poor man to the hospital and he erupted furiously. 'Who can I call to the hospital at this hour? You know I am on leave. Tell them to go to Dr Sen.'

'How can you say this?' Jayanti was livid. 'I don't care if you are on leave or not—you have to take him there.' When she gave orders, everyone listened to Jayanti, I can tell you.

Her husband tried to wriggle out saying, 'I'll take him in the morning. Tell them to go and sleep in Daulat's room.'

'I'll assist you.' Jayanti would not be dissuaded. 'And you know perfectly well that Daulat won't allow even a bird to share his room.'

She was absolutely right. Daulat was a part of my mother's huge retinue, now with Jayanti. For twenty-five years, he had spread terror in my mother's household. Finally, she could take no more of his filthy temper and packed him off to Jayanti's house. Daulat's effeminate ways were the talk of the town and, when he draped his dhoti over his head and snaked his way down a road, people would openly titter at him. My elder brother used to call him Damyanti but with a temper like his, perhaps Durvasa would have been a more appropriate nickname! He ruled over Jayanti's kitchen like a tyrant and his waspish tongue could flay the skin off someone's face. When Jayanti lost her favourite pen, she sent someone to ask Daulat whether he had seen it. 'Yes,' was the reply sent through the trembling courier, 'tell her I am signing the chapattis with it!'

There was no question of Daulat allowing anyone access to his room at that hour of the night. So my brother-in-law, Jayanti and I stumbled with the injured man and his wife to the hospital in the freezing cold at two-thirty in the morning. 'Where is the nose?' my brother-in-law asked.

'Here,' said the wife and carefully unwrapped it from a fig leaf. It took some two or three hours to suture the nose back on to the man's face and I was amazed at my brother-in-law's courage in tackling the job, without proper assistance, no lights and just his wife and a hysterical twosome as audience. Would any modern surgeon even dare to take on such a job? Miraculously, the man recovered, and why not? How could there have been any chance of an infection when nature itself had sanitized the whole atmosphere with a thick blanket of snow?

Two years later, the grateful patient returned, a huge grin under his restored nose. In his hand were two containers for the doctor and his wife—one with fragrant honey and the other brimming with pure ghee from his village.

Another time, the X-ray technician lost his wife at a game of cards. The poor girl, a pretty young thing, came sobbing to Jayanti. 'Save my honour, Dactrani-jyu,' she wailed. 'This bastard has sold me for three thousand rupees!' The perpetrator of the crime stood next to her, weeping and speechless with shame. Jayanti saved his wife but forbade her to go back to her husband. She arranged to have her trained as a nurse and gave her an income to live a life of honour and independence. Years later, I used the incident to write a story called 'Piti Hui Gote'.

Then came the doe-eyed Bhagirathi—slim, sultry and siren-like. Married to an alcoholic much older than her, who used to beat her every day taunting her childlessness by saying, 'Whore, you haven't even produced a mouse in the four years we have been married,' Bhagirathi ran away and arrived at Jayanti's doorstep. Dressed in the ghagra-choli of a village belle, she was quite an attractive bundle. My mother took one look at her and said sharply, 'Jayanti, pack her off right away, I tell you. Otherwise you will regret your generosity. I don't like the look of her—her nara is dangling and that, my child, is the sign of a harlot.'

But once Jayanti made up her mind, could anyone persuade her to change it? Within a year, Bhagirathi became a different thing. Her large eyes were lined with kohl, her hair sported a saucy red flower and the ghagra was replaced with a sari with a jaunty pallu that fluttered with every step she took. I renamed her Sujata, after the famous Bimal Roy film of those days, because she reminded me of the actress Nutan.

My mother's prophecy proved true. Sujata first fluttered her eyes in the direction of my mother's house. My elder brother's cook, a handsome young man called Dilip, was her first victim. When the vegetables started to burn, Jayanti realized that she must cut short her visit to my mother's house before worse things happened. Sujata was taken away but her lover could not bear her betrayal and Dilip committed suicide. Eventually, her husband and children told Jayanti that Sujata must leave. Jayanti agreed reluctantly but got her a job as a gram sevika before abandoning her to her own devices. She was followed by another

131

siren and, finally, Jayanti vowed never to take on the cause of young women. Then, as if to test her promise, a mad woman landed up at her doorstep and refused to leave. She would lie around the veranda, singing, dancing and generally entertaining the house. Apparently, her husband's affair with another woman had turned her mind crazy. 'I stole all the jewellery and wear a loincloth, hahaha…' she told Jayanti one day and vanished. A few days later, they found her body on the streets. After her came a leper from Bhimtal—he was installed under an apple tree in the garden. 'I know Dr Moses of the Almora Leper Asylum,' I told Jayanti. 'Let me send him there—you must think of your children and husband too.'

'No.'

It had been like this with her ever since she was at school. When we were in Gujarat, my mother had adopted an orphan girl called Panchi Bai. The village headman had left her in my mother's care after she lost her parents in a flood, so my mother became her 'Ba' (mother in Gujarati).

'Ba,' Panchi Bai declared one day, 'I want a man.'

The whole house was stunned at this shameless declaration. All except Jayanti, of course, who went and found her a suitable boy, another orphan called Jiwaram. One day, Jiwaram arrived resplendent in a saffron turban and stood with folded hands before my mother to seek Panchi Bai's hand.

Jiwaram had no home and no job. 'How will you look after her?' my mother asked this hopeless suitor. He looked bashfully at the ground and replied, 'Annadata, you are there, aren't you?' So Panchi Bai was married—my mother gave her the dowry she would give a daughter and the barat started at our front door and went round the house to end at the kitchen door. Jiwaram was given driving lessons (Jayanti organized that, of course) and became our driver.

When we went to Tikamgarh, Jayanti picked up a girl called Lalita, who had just one good eye. When her husband abandoned her for this reason, Jayanti took her in hand. She groomed her, taught her and, within a year, Lalita was a changed girl. One day, her husband saw her at a fair, fell in love with her and took her back!

Meanwhile, in Rajkot, Jiwaram and Panchi Bai embarked on Project Family with such enthusiasm that within a few years there were several children—Popat, Radhabai and god knows who else. Then, tragedy struck and Jiwaram died of TB. Where else could poor Panchi Bai go but to her Ba's home? She arrived with her football team and stayed on for thirty years, travelling with us from Bangalore to Almora or wherever my father's work took us. Finally, she retired to her beloved Kutch.

After my father's sudden death, Jayanti became the head of the family. Our education, our travels across the country—all became her responsibility. Sometimes I wonder how she did it all. Yet I always knew that she was a born mother and that ultimately she would not be able to resist domestic bliss. Years ago, worried about her vow of celibacy, I had asked a mendicant who used to visit us from time to time. 'Yes, your sister will marry one day,' she had said emphatically to me.

Jayanti married someone of her own choice but in her inimitable style, and after great opposition from the family. My brother-in-law was a handsome surgeon, westernized in his education and bearing. He had had a brush with tuberculosis in his younger days. TB was considered a curse then, a sure sign of early death but Jayanti cared for no one's advice. She and her husband were devoted to each other and when she lost him a few years ago, she lost her own will to live.

After her husband's death she only visited me once or twice and when she came to Lucknow to receive an award from the

Hindi Sansthan, all our time went remembering the past. It was on the same trip that two of her Buddhist friends came visiting. The two monks had travelled from Gorakhpur to ask her to read two manuscripts in the Kharoshti script, which she did in minutes, translating them effortlessly into Sanskrit. On a trip to Kathmandu, she composed a Sanskrit hymn in praise of Pashupatinath and gave that to the priest as an offering. At the age of seventy-five, she trudged up 14,000 feet to visit the temple of Tunganath and recited some rare Sanskrit slokas to the priest who fell at her feet. 'Ma, you are Saraswati,' he said to her in awe.

'No, not Saraswati, Pujari-jyu,' she replied, 'just her devotee.' The more I remember what she was, the more I feel Jayanti was, in Tagore's words, a river that lost its way in the sand.

She was in unbearable pain in her last days. Her feet were swollen, for her kidneys had failed, and she would float in and out of consciousness to look around her restlessly when she was awake. I stayed a few days and then when I went to say goodbye to her before leaving for Lucknow, my eyes filled up. She could recognize me but her sad eyes were dry. I think the searing pain of one's last few days dries up all one's tears. And that sad face, shrunken and forlorn, is the one that floats before my eyes when I recall her now.

With time, I feel, relationships have changed radically. I don't see in this generation the love we had for our siblings. We fought and said cruel things to each other but when it was time to part we felt as if a limb had been cut off. My sister Manjula and her husband had moved in with Jayanti to look after her but she was away that day. So was Jayanti's devoted son, Pushpesh, who had to go to the university for a lecture. So she and I spent one last day together. She bared her heart for the first and last time that day. Her loneliness after her husband's death, and what it was like for her to be cut off from her children's lives and the world around her—all this and more...

'You had once written in some story that a man's umbilical cord is cut twice—once when he leaves his mother's womb and the second time when he gets married,' she smiled and pressed my hand gently. That touch said more than a thousand words to me.

Finally, it was time to leave her.

'Jayanti, I am going,' I said softly. She looked at me with unseeing eyes and turned her head away. She had withdrawn from this world already.

I am told she returned to her old self a few days before she died. But I am haunted by that last goodbye—her touch transferred all her pain to me that day. Lying alone in a house, no loved ones around her, all she did was live in the past. Santiniketan, Shillong, Bangalore, Orchcha, Rajkot... Do you remember, she asked me that day, Ija's sweet voice singing:

Aaj to sapna ma mane
Dolna dungar divyajo...
(I dreamt of the rolling mountains today...)

With death hovering over her head, I am sure she could see the mountains we saw from our grandfather's courtyard in Almora—Kamet, Nanda Devi, Trisul, Banari Devi...

God knows what pain she took with her when she died. And perhaps it was this that took her mind into a peculiar direction. She began to take an unhealthy interest in other people's lives, a weakness cruelly exploited by some relatives. They would first encourage her to talk ill of someone, then it would be spiced up and spread around. So one often heard 'Jayanti said this or that about you...she's become senile...' and so on. But how many, I wonder, saw her brilliance? Or her heart that was as clean as a mirror? So generous, that she gave away all she had to whoever asked for it. Did anyone ever realize that she gave away so much that finally she had nothing left for herself? They stopped giving her money because she spent whatever she had in hand. She had already donated all her pension—yet she swore that a yogi had once given her a 'magic tortoise' that would always keep her in clover.

'Touch a copper penny to it and it will turn into silver,' he had told her. We used to titter behind her back but nevertheless went furtively to touch its metal back. I myself tried it many times, and I have to tell you it worked. Some forgotten royalty cheque or other would land up after that magic touch.

A few months before her death, knowing how she yearned for the old days, I told her, 'Jayanti, you have a cottage in Bhowali. Why don't you go back there? Isn't it better than lying alone here in Delhi? I may be younger than you but even I know one does not die of any disease—it is the memories of the past that eventually kill you.'

She smiled through cracked lips, and that smile went like a dagger to my heart. She took my hand in her trembling and feverish clasp and whispered:

Sar sookhe, pachchi ure aure saran samae
Deen meen bin pachch ke, kahu Rahim kahan jaye?
(Birds fly from a drying lake to seek another perch
But where, O Rahim, shall a wingless fish flee?)

8

Hamid Bhai

As I translated one article after another, fascinated by the life that was unfolding in another language, I realized that there could be nothing modest about this book. Diddi had always commanded total attention and, even when she was alive, she had the capacity to use up all the oxygen in a room. Now, she leapt at me from every line that she had written. So many characters and events I encountered were familiar and everywhere, beneath the surface of the written word, I could see a history that was ours as much as it was hers. True, Diddi had made us into what we were but it was equally true that we had made her into what she was. Yet I constantly worried whether in writing of her I was getting distracted into writing about us, not her. Before me was a giant jigsaw puzzle—a nose peeped from one corner and a leg from another—where should I start to begin piecing them together?

My task was not made easier by Diddi's restless writing style. Not for nothing had we nicknamed her Virginia Woolf because she was known to destroy a conversation by suddenly asking a question or introducing a subject that had nothing to do with the matters being discussed. Worse, she would get up abruptly and leave a bewildered roomful of people behind. Telephone conversations with her were hell—she used the telephone as a means of passing on or receiving urgent news. If there was none, she could not bear to waste her time on inane 'So what's happening?' kind of chatter. 'Click', and the line went dead, your conversation was cut off, for she had heard and said all she wanted to hear or say. When I started to translate her work, I found myself struggling to keep the narrative going in a coherent, orderly progression. More often than not, an idea or character would emerge, begin to acquire flesh and shape and, suddenly, Diddi would be off at another tangent because she remembered another story, another episode that she had to squeeze in. It was exhausting to keep pace with such a mind.

And then there was the mystery of her pseudonym, Shivani. 'Shivani' at first seemed a mask that gave her an assurance because of its anonymity but, as I read on, I realized it was much, much more. Diddi was actually two people, and she used the two personas as identical twins do: to confuse and confound. Like them, she had mastered the art of switching from one to the other so seamlessly that even she did not know any more who she was. So the person she was, the person she wanted to be and the person that, unknown to all of us, she really was was someone called Gaura, Diddi, Nani, Dadi, Bahuji and Shivani. And yet, there was a core of Diddi that remained inviolate and secret all her life. She hid her fears and pain from everyone— even herself. Her writing was for her a way of recording people and events that she could not bear to speak about. Diddi was a master in the art of hiding her grief. Some of it she buried in her writing; the rest she buried inside her. Her writing was thus a huge ruse to keep her pain away from those whose pity she did not want yet she left this pain for some of us to discover.

After Babu died in 1974, Diddi was allotted a flat in Lucknow as an accredited journalist and she started writing a weekly column for one of the local newspapers. The subjects she chose ranged from local issues of civic concern to musings on life, or interesting characters she had come across, obituaries, and reviews of concerts and recitals. Week after week, whether ill or well, she churned out these columns because they gave her a roof over her head. The column called 'Jalak', or window, became hugely popular and it reached out to a vast readership. From college teachers to her milkman, her fan following grew day by day. There was no place, whether a bank or a shop, where people would not rise reverently to greet her when they saw her. An interesting incident illustrates her popularity among her fans best. Diddi was once travelling to Delhi by train from Lucknow and reached the station only to discover that she had forgotten her box of tobacco (she was addicted to perfumed chewing tobacco). She reached her compartment and the ticket collector came to greet her, for he had seen her name on the reservation chart. 'If there is anything I can do, Shivaniji,' he folded his hands as he got up to prepare for the departure of the train in a few minutes, 'just call me.'

'Now that you say so,' replied Diddi, 'I wonder if you could get me a pouch of tobacco from the station shop. You see,' she told him disarmingly, 'I can't last till the morning without it.'

'At once,' the man said and went personally to fetch it.

'And he delayed the departure of the Lucknow Mail by five minutes,' she told me proudly when she arrived, 'so that he could fetch me my tobacco!'

At the same time, she wrote short stories, travelogues and serials to earn enough to live by. Babu and she had married the daughters off, but they were left with virtually nothing for their old age. But it was beneath Diddi to seek help or pity. Like Ama, selling off the family silver to keep the family afloat, Diddi hawked her talent to earn enough for herself and the families of the helpers she had around her. They ate what she ate, lived as she did and shared her life more completely than any of us imagined.

Thus it was that for nearly thirty years, Diddi became a fixture in Lucknow's Gulistan Colony: every child and resident there knew who she was. She hardly ever visited her neighbours, but she always knew that when the need arose she could depend on them. In a sense, they became her surrogate family. A daughter-in-law from a nearby flat would come to Diddi to complain about her mother-in-law and a little later the mother-in-law would follow with her tale of woes. Every Holi, the entire colony would come to her to wish her and she made huge quantities of gujiyas specially for them. The vendors and workers came to her for loans, for a rest and a cup of tea. Their lives nourished her and dispelled the loneliness of a mother too proud to tell her children she was tired of living alone. Over time, we all began to believe that she actually preferred to stay in her crumbling flat—or perhaps it suited us to believe this myth of the fearless matriarch who preferred to live alone. She often joked that a new neighbour once asked her, 'Shivaniji, are you childless?' because we started visiting her less and less. Instead, she would dutifully come and spend time with each one of us.

There was another reason for Diddi's withdrawal from us as we grew older. This stemmed from her inability to confront adult problems. She always had a special affinity with children—whether her own or those that were attracted to her warmth and lively personality. Yet when they grew up and developed into difficult adolescents and adults, Diddi ran away from their problems. 'Don't tell me,' she often said when one of us embarked on a particular problem in our lives. 'I can't bear to hear of your unhappiness.' She hated being exposed to the pain of the ones she loved the most and several times I had to almost drag her to visit an ailing cousin or aunt. In her own life, as in her writing, Diddi was the quintessential escapist.

Yet I know of no other person who could laugh at herself (and others) with such openness and who had such a perfect crap detector. I like to think this is a gift that Diddi passed on to all of us, even my children. Whenever she came to visit one of us, she brought such cheer and laughter that even our servants would beg her to extend her stay. It was a joke with us that Diddi came with a small overnighter when she came to visit us. For the time she was with one of her daughters, she loved wearing our saris because she was fed up with hers and gave them away readily so that she could be rid of something that had no novelty for her any more. It was also her way of letting us know that she was here for just a few days: her real home was elsewhere.

The day started with her puja—she sang beautifully as she bathed her gods. Her voice rang over the house as she ordered her tea and newspapers and we woke up. The cook was told what to make and how to make it and pickles, chutneys, sweets that were laden with forbidden calories came out of our kitchens long starved of such rich food. The grandchildren pestered her for stories that were told night after night as serials through her visit. She loved spoiling her grandchildren—encouraging them to swear and deliberately said irreverent, un-grandmotherly things to shock and amuse them. In the evenings, the servants sat around her as she watched TV, making rude remarks about political figures to their huge amusement. 'This one's mother or father,' she said once looking at a well-known politician with prominent teeth, 'was definitely a rabbit.' Among her regular

TV viewing was the programme that flashed the faces of people lost and found. For some odd reason, she watched each face intently and often commented, 'This one is better lost.' And then looked around for the round of laughter and applause that inevitably followed. In short, she cultivated the persona of a clown and entertainer to deflect attention from the overwhelming question that haunted her: how long would she be able to stay alone in Lucknow? And when the time came for her to be cared for by someone, where would she go?

She never came as close to voicing these fears as in an article she wrote on the death of Hamid Bhai, her friend and surrogate brother. His lonely death frightened her: she herself was a diabetic, had had several close shaves—a burst appendix followed by peritonitis and tubercular glands in her neck. What if she were to slip into a coma and none of the children were near? In a rare moment of seriousness, she once told me, 'I don't want to get used to such love as I find in your homes. Nor do I want to get accustomed to air-conditioned rooms. When I am here and see the tensions in all your lives, I want to run back to Lucknow and live my solitary life. If I don't see you all, I know you are well. But just picture me as I enter my house when I return to Lucknow. As I open my front door, I shut my eyes against the stench of an old, crumbling house. I can't sleep many nights and lie awake thinking of you all—I hope Minu is less stressed, I hope Micky is not travelling in a plane that may crash, I hope you are sleeping enough and I hope Binu eases up on worrying eternally... When I am not with you all, you all are with me. All the time.'

This could have been Ama writing to Diddi: Diddi was slowly morphing into Ama.

~

My Brother

An obituary by Diddi (late 1970s):

… This time I returned to Lucknow the day before Eid. I waited for a long time for Hamid Bhai to arrive for it had never happened that he did not visit me on Eid, carrying a bowl of sevian wrapped clumsily in a kerchief. And this was a man who had no kitchen to call his own. He lived alone in a hotel, yet whenever his friends or relatives sent him sevian on Eid, he would carefully keep aside a portion for me. I can never forget the taste of that bowl of sevian, a combination of many flavours, redolent with the aroma of so many kitchens. When he did not arrive this time, it struck me as ominous that he had not replied to my letter written from Bombay. Something was wrong, I thought, and quickly called up a mutual friend. 'Oh, didn't you hear? He passed away this May,' she said. 'He went to sleep one night and just never woke up.'

I was numb with guilt. Why had I kept silent after writing him just one letter from Bombay? After all, I could have written to someone else and asked about him. He and I may not have been born of one womb but would I ever find a brother like him again? My brother had gone, my brain kept repeating, and I did not know till now.

Every Holi Hamid Bhai came to my house to eat gujiyas even though he hated the festival. '*Lahaul vila quvat!*' he spat in disgust. 'What kind of festival do you Hindus call this? Here I was in my white achkan, but do you think that stopped those goons from spraying me with some vile colour? May the bastards rot in hell!' When my husband was seriously ill, he came silently to sit at his bedside. 'Go,' he would tell me kindly. 'Do what you have to—I'm here to look after him.' Often I would keep him

143

there for hours as I combed little-known shops tracking down ingredients to concoct the potions my husband's Ayurvedic doctor had prescribed: ashwagandha, punarnava and god knows what other herbs. I would return sheepishly to find Hamid Bhai sitting patiently waiting for me. When even those potions failed to save my husband's life, I felt as if I was adrift, alone in a dark world. My relatives dispersed as rapidly as a crowd after a street show is over, to avoid shelling out money, I suppose. There was just Hamid Bhai who was always there for me. 'Look, child,' he put his hand on my shoulder, 'if you don't keep your chin up, there is no hope. Put this behind you and move on. Inshallah, He will lend you a hand.'

When I look back to those dark days, I realize I was given my armour by Hamid Bhai, and my weapons for survival by Nagarji, who said, 'I want you to live with your head held high—not weeping and whining.' My patience came from my guru, Hajari Prasad Dwivedi, who quoted a line in Sanskrit to the effect that adversity lends one patience, his eyes streaming with tears as he blessed me with this sloka.

My first memories of Hamid Bhai are from our childhood in Rampur, the golden years of my life. I remember Khas Bagh, Mustafa Lodge, Rose Villa, Meena Bazar, and the gifts that Dawn and Wali Ahad, the nawab's children, used to send us. Our servants swim next before my eyes: Chaman Khan, Munne Khan, Sikander Mian, Jumman, Muhammad Ali Peshkar and my father's steno, Alawi Sahib. I remember the fragrance of hina and shamatulambar, and beautiful eyes peering at us from behind the lace eyelets of a burqa. Our house, Mustafa Lodge, was a huge bungalow and my father was the first Hindu home minister of the state. Hamid Bhai's uncle Sir Abdul Samad Khan's house, Rose Villa, was next door. Hamid Bhai was the second son of Abdul Wahid Khan. He had no sisters of his own, so he adopted us girls as his own. I must have been about eight or ten years old then. Whenever he came home for his vacations, he would bring me a gift—a beautiful dress, or a doll or crackers from the Army and Navy Stores that showered little gifts on us when we pulled them apart. And on Eid! No matter which corner of the world he was in, Hamid Bhai never forgot to send me ten rupees as my Eidi. He was such a dandy in those days. My father once warned my mother that as Hamid was coming for tea, she had better make sure it was served properly. Hamid Bhai had just come back from abroad and was a little particular about these niceties.

In looks, Hamid Bhai was the exact opposite of his handsome father: dark, with a long nose and huge hairy nostrils, hooded eyes that always appeared half-closed, thick, fleshy lips, short and very, very fat. When he sat on a sofa, it would groan as it sank under his weight; when he laughed you would think a bolt of cloth was being ripped. And yet he had an aura of elegance about him. I remember he once took us children for a drive in his gleaming new Morris to Bilaspur tehsil. Along with us on the seat sat a many-domed tiffin carrier and a hamper with white, starched napkins and cutlery that you could see yourself in. When we sat down to our picnic, we were terrified that we'd pick the wrong fork and watched him to pick the right one in case we disgraced ourselves.

Sadly, I was also a witness to the twilight of his life. He lived in Room Number Two of Burlington Hotel in Lucknow, a Shah Jahan trapped in a cell. Peeling plaster on the walls, cobwebs swinging from the skylights, a sagging bed with a carelessly thrown cheap bedcover that half-covered its spotted sheets and a depressing, dank air that suffocated one's throat. I found him once eating off an enamel plate, which had leathery chapattis, and a pair of chipped bowls with some watery dal and rice.

As I watched him eat that day, I recalled an entry from his diary he had given me to read once:

> The nawab sahib used to be seated on a divan that had silver legs and every guest to the meal had an appointed place. My uncle was given a place of honour as the nawab's general. The food was served in large round silver plates and came in courses: first came two kinds of salan, seekh kababs and pulao. Then sweet rice and phirni. Several bearers would stand holding silver goblets, their mouths covered with a red cloth and stamped with a seal. Each time, the nawab sahib asked for water, a court official would break the seal and as the nawab took his first sip the hall would resound with a loud 'Bismillah, ur-Rehman.'

Had Hamid Bhai been able to erase the memory of those royal meals I wondered as I saw his pathetic fare that day. 'Join me?' he asked and then in the next breath, 'God forgive me, child, how can I even ask you to share this swill?'

Every Sunday, he would eat his lunch with me. He had spent a long time in the hills, so was very partial to Kumaoni food. Each Sunday, at his special request, I cooked him a 'Garampani meal': hot round puris, yellow potato sabzi and a tangy raita made with cucumbers and a touch of mustard. Gradually, he became weaker, developed some heart trouble and his knees started to trouble him as well. He would drag himself upstairs to my flat somehow but, later, even hauling himself out of the rickshaw became difficult. Yet worse than the betrayal of his body was the betrayal of the relatives he had loved. His nephews, whose expensive school education he had funded, went away to settle abroad. His father died in an accident and his younger brother, incarcerated for years in a mental asylum, died as well.

Suddenly, all his family seemed to have deserted Hamid Bhai and he was left all alone in the world. He realized then that many of them had merely made use of him when he had something to give: when the money ran out, so did they. This turned him in his last days into a misanthrope and he took to cursing them whenever he found a listener: 'So-and-so did not take me to that walima; that one did not reply to my letter; such-and-such Chachi came to Lucknow and did not even care to visit me; my nephews write, come to us, we will send you a ticket—and it's been three years since that offer. Bastards! Do they have the balls to send a ticket? Even if they sent one now, I would tear it and chuck it out of the window!'

His pride forbade him to seek pity. As I read through his diary, I realized why:

Jalaluddin Khan and Sadaullah Khan had been shot for their participation in the 1857 revolt. This Sadaullah Khan was my grandfather. After his death, his wife Qudsia Begum took her family to Rampur, whose nawab, Yusuf Khan, was her kin. The nawab had recently been decorated with the title of farzand-e-dil-pazir-daulat-e-inglisia by the British, with whom he had a cordial relationship. How could he possibly give sanctuary to the hot-blooded Rohilla family of Qudsia Begum? My grandmother was a woman of great dignity and sagacity. The minute she sensed the nawab's hesitation, she quietly left with her family for Moradabad…

The same Pathani blood ran in Hamid Bhai's veins to the end. I also knew why Hamid Bhai had taken a vow of celibacy. The one he wanted to marry had ditched him despite many promises of undying love for him. Then she married someone else and migrated to Pakistan. In his last days, this came back to haunt him and one day, after ages, she suddenly arrived to visit him unannounced. He came straight to me after he saw her off. 'Child, she came today!' His face had a flushed look as he announced this.

'Who?' I asked.

'Who else?' he laughed sadly and recited:

My youth is long past, yet
The pain of love
Hurts as sharply now
As it did then.

'That one,' he elaborated. 'Came from Pakistan.' How could I have been so obtuse the first time, I thought. 'Why didn't you stop her, Hamid Bhai?' I asked. 'I believe she is a widow now.'

'My dear,' he said, after a long sigh. 'When I had a strong voice and a heart that beat, I couldn't stop her. Do you think she would hear me today when I can hardly hear myself? As for my heart, I have given it to Dr Mansur [his cardiologist] now. Once I loved three things: good food, good drink and good clothes. Life seems to have taken them all away from me.'

I was witness to all these three loves. He had had to quit drinking a long time ago, Mansur Mian had made him give up good food and his tight purse strings took away the good clothes as well. Who could say looking at him in his later years that Hamid Bhai's clothes once came from Phelps', his shoes were polished for hours and whenever he went on a tour, his valet would scurry behind him carrying a bag with shoe polish and brushes to clean them after every ten steps. You could smell his aftershave from a mile off. And now? Torn socks and ancient gloves with three fingers peeping from the holes in them. I

148

knitted him a new pair but he lost them. His huge body was stuffed somehow into the rickshaw and reminded me of the enormous quilts we used to stuff into holdalls when travelling, worried that the belt would give way! Patched clothes flapping about him, he would call from the road outside my house: 'Child! Are you home?'

In the last year, he could not even get down from the rickshaw and I would take his thali down to the rickshaw to feed him. Then, he did not even have the strength to eat properly and I used to worry that if something were to happen to him outside my flat, on the street, what would I do? To make matters worse, he had now become like a Lear—demented with grief and sorrow. He forgot who was dead and who was alive. 'Go, call them down!' he would command me. 'Tribhi, Shukdeo—where are they? I have come all this way to meet them. Why can't they come down to meet me?'

When I reminded him gently that my brother Tribhi and my husband had gone, he would say, Gone where? Why can't you go and call them? I wish I could, Hamid Bhai, I'd reply. Then go! I am ordering you to, the old Pathan would thunder. No one can go there, Hamid Bhai—not even a farzand-e-dil-pazir daulat-e-inglisia, I once tried a weak joke. He became livid. 'You have the audacity to laugh? I'll knock your teeth in if you do that again. Go, call them!' Curtains twitched in my neighbourhood and curious eyes and ears strained to hear the string of curses that Hamid Bhai then hurled at me. To me, these were like the curses that a Sufi fakir hurls to the heavens to have them return as blessing on him—but who would believe that? His old rickshawallah—whom Hamid Bhai called his friend, philosopher and guide—shook his head sadly, 'Sahibzada has gone crazy, bahuji,' he said. 'Allah Mian should call him now. He has done so much for me, bahuji, that I cannot thank him enough. He took me to see *Pakeezah* twenty-five times, and made me sit in the box with him! Was there a single film that the Sahibzada ever missed?'

Films were his obsession—he often sat through three consecutive shows. Then, when that too became impossible, Hamid Bhai became a fakir. He wandered about the lanes of Lucknow in a rickshaw—Mahanagar, Nishatganj, Nakkhas, Aminabad: each locality had someone he knew but they began to shun him after a point. He came to me one day and I was in my puja so it took me a little while to go down to him sprawled in his rickshaw. He'll curse, I was worried, but that day, the river of fire had cooled to a different mood. His forlorn face and brimming eyes accused me silently. Could I not have cut short my puja for once, I thought guiltily. This was the man who I would race down to receive as a child, 'What did you bring for me?' and today I had made this old, old man wait for me! 'Forgive me, Hamid Bhai, I was doing my puja…' my voice tapered off.

He was sunk in silence.

I went forward and held his hand and it was as if that touch led to a dam burst. I had never seen him cry, let alone sob. Who had hurt him today, I wondered. 'Is all well, Hamid Bhai? What happened?' I asked.

'What can I say, child? There were just two homes that I thought were mine—yours and Chachi's. Today I was turned away from there—Chachi told me very clearly, I don't think you should come here in this condition, Hamid.'

His favourite cousin had recently written to him that she didn't think it was wise for him to visit her in Aligarh any more. What if something happened to him while on a train? And even if you were to come here, I don't think I can look after you, she had written. You know how busy I am with my medical practice—I just can't think of handling another sick person.

'There you are, so now my sister thinks of me not as a brother but as a potential patient!' he laughed and quoted: 'The minute the walls of my humble home fell, / People rushed in to make it a thoroughfare.'

The Pakistani Foreign Minister Sahibzada Yaqub Khan was his first cousin. One day, I told him, 'How similar your faces are, Hamid Bhai!' 'That's all that's alike, my dear,' he replied sadly. 'Our destinies were very different.'

The minute I mentioned that I would be travelling out of Lucknow, his face would fall. 'When you are away, I feel so lonely, child. Suppose I die when you are not here, who will take me to my grave?'

'Go on, Hamid Bhai,' I laughed, 'I can only take you to the cremation ground. How can you forget that you are a Muslim and I a Hindu?'

He flashed me a look of such anger that my smile died on my lips. 'Stop this nonsense! I am not a Muslim nor are you a Hindu—I don't believe in your temple and you don't believe in my mosque. Just remember one truth, child, you are my sister and I am your brother. This relationship will always endure.'

And he remained my brother to the end of his life. He came to every daughter's wedding. Each of my sons-in-law touched his feet. And when my daughter-in-law's mother sent him an expensive pullover as a gift, his eyes filled up with tears.

This March when he came to see me, I noticed his feet were swollen. He was almost incoherent and would lapse into the past. As he was leaving, he said, 'Child, this is our last meeting. I will never see you again.' Then he took my hand in his swollen fingers and touched it to his forehead. My throat was so tight that I could not speak, then I swallowed my tears and said, 'How can you say this, Hamid Bhai? I will come a day before Eid for my Eidi.'

But I reached too late to get that Eidi. He had once told me, 'Never fear Death. Look at me, both my feet are in the grave and the minute I hear Allah Mian, I'll jump right into it. Remember that Death only tortures cowards—the mouse fears the cat, so the cat loves to torture it before it kills it. Those who don't fear Death are borne triumphantly on its shoulders.'

And that is how he went. God knows in which lane of Lucknow he sleeps now. One day, I swear, I will find it out and tell the Angel of Death that here lies a man who said that nothing was dearer to him than our relationship—he was my brother and I his sister. Nothing else endured.

9

Ramrati

If there was one grace that Diddi lacked, it was accepting help from anyone—even her children. Any hint of pity, a note of compassion in someone's voice made her curl up her lip and bare her fangs. This often pushed those whom she loved the most very far from her. Worse, in her last years, when she wanted someone to take her in, warts and all, she only succeeded in pushing them away. Diddi had always been fiercely independent, so, like Ama, she chose to live alone rather than seek help or a shelter from those she could not live comfortably with. Eventually, this independence developed into an almost destructive streak. Despite many pleas from all of us to wind up her Lucknow house and move in with one of us, Diddi refused to budge from her crumbling flat in Gulistan Colony. Life had taught her never to trust anyone but herself and her fragile sense of dignity was quick to take offence. She also knew that she could not inflict her laws on her children, and that she could not submit to a lifestyle that did not have her sanction. So her final years were spent in Lucknow, and her flat there became a retreat in the same way that Kasoon had become one for Ama. She became Ama—a lonely matriarch trapped in a deserted home. Lear had his Fool, Ama had Tara Didi, and Diddi had Ramrati.

Servants had always played a very important role in Diddi's life just as they had in Ama's. The servants in Diddi's home, as in Ama's, were never taught to serve tea correctly or picked for their skills in household matters. They were chosen because they were one of a kind and encouraged to be sassy and exit with perfect lines from a room. In our childhood, almost all the servants who worked with us were children of Ama's old servants and, since they had seen us grow up, they participated in our lives as equals. They stayed on for years and when they died or retired, their children came to take their place. Ramrati, my mother's maid of many years, was celebrated with an article on her when she died and her daughter Kiran and her children were my mother's constant companions till her death. They ate with her, slept in the other bedroom and called her Diddi or Nani, just as we did. Fittingly, it was Kiran's face that was displayed in all Diddi's last pictures because she sat cradling my mother's head on her lap before they took her away. When a pesky photographer was contorting his body to get the most poignant picture of Diddi at her funeral, Kiran told me, 'When Amritlal Nagar died, I went with Diddi. A photographer toppled off and almost fell on Nagarji's body. Diddi asked him loudly, "*Kyon bhai, Nagarji ke sath upar jaane ka iraada hai?*"' (Do you wish to go up there with Nagarji?) Then, trained perfectly by my mother, Kiran walked up to the photographer and said, '*Ab aap jaiyey*.' (Please leave now.)

The house that Diddi and Ramrati lived in was like no other that I know of. For one, there was complete democracy in Diddi's house. Master and servant had the same rights and were equal in every respect. Ramrati's family became Diddi's loyal band of helpers and this clan grew into an army of some twenty-odd people. Ramrati's married daughters came every weekend with their children to meet Diddi. They brought her tales from their lives and Diddi was deeply involved in the politics of their homes. Prema's husband was a drunkard and beat her. 'Slap him back,' Diddi advised the weeping Prema and then summoned him one morning to give him a piece of her mind. She got Prema trained as a midwife and once Prema became independent of him, she regained her courage to take him on. I think she even slapped him, much to Diddi's delight. Another faithful weekend visitor was Misrilal, the dhobi. A thin, wiry man who cycled some 15 miles to come every week, Misrilal was a comical figure who wore khaki shorts that flapped in the breeze as he cycled. 'He used to come,' my son says, 'to spend the day with Nani.' The minute Misrilal came, he was greeted warmly by the kitchen staff and given a refreshing drink and told to rest in the veranda. Often he dozed for a couple of hours before he went into the house. Then he came into Diddi's room and squatted on the floor as he narrated his woes: his only son had gone away to Bombay to join the film world and his daughter-in-law was a shrew who tortured poor Misrilal. The saga of Misrilal's domestic woes were related like a weekly TV soap to Diddi, who listened intently to every detail and offered advice or solace.

Then, suddenly, Misrilal stopped coming and no one knew what had happened. Diddi was left without a dhobi and the absence began to show. On a visit to Lucknow, I found the bedsheets so grubby that I asked her why she did not consider finding a replacement for Misrilal. 'There are no dhobis in Lucknow any more,' Diddi replied.

'How can that be?' I asked. 'There are at least a dozen in the colony, aren't there?'

'There were, you mean,' Diddi smiled. 'Now they've all become ministers.'

This is when Mayawati, the great champion of the lower

castes, had been elected chief minister of Uttar Pradesh for the first time and presided over a strange cabinet of ministers who she had chosen not for their aptitude but their caste. Diddi had no belief in politically correct language and freely aired her views to her appreciative audience. On another occasion, someone came to her to unveil a statue of the great champion of the lower castes Dr Ambedkar. Anyone who has seen any statue of the venerable nationalist will remember that he is always depicted as wearing trousers that stop at his ankles. Diddi excused herself from the honour: 'I am not well nowadays,' she lied. 'My doctors have forbidden me to travel. But do me a favour, will you?' she asked the supplicant. 'Take some money from me and just add two inches to his trouser length before you get someone to unveil the poor man's statue.'

Interestingly, in her real life she was completely free of all caste biases. Her old sweeper Mohan and his wife, Bahuriya, were valued members of her court and sipped tea with the other servants. Every time Diddi returned to Lucknow, she took the brightest sari and bangles for Bahuriya. Years ago, Diddi had got her a job as a sweeper in the railways but Bahuriya still came every morning to sweep the terrace and have her morning tea with Diddi before she went on her 'dooty'. Then there was Burho, the old crone who came to massage Diddi. Burho was a childless widow and had found her way into Diddi's durbar. She ate her meals there and went home only to sleep. My children used to tease Diddi saying that she should be the one massaging Burho, considering how frail Burho was. When Burho died, she had asked that her bier be taken past Diddi's house and Diddi paid for the funeral as she had promised, showering rose petals on the bier as it went past her house. The scene was not unlike Queen Elizabeth standing outside Buckingham Palace bowing to the funeral cortege of Princess

Diana! We used to joke that Diddi, like the Government of India, provided cradle to grave security to her workers. In the last few years, she donated all the award money she received either to Mother Teresa or to one of the workers.

Yet of all the servants, it was Ramrati who remained my mother's favourite and who served her until she died. After her death, her daughter Kiran became Diddi's surrogate child and remained with her till the very end. Even now, she never forgets to call us up on our birthdays and anniversaries and rings me up every Sunday. But the person who missed Ramrati the most was her husband, Phainku. After she died, he took on her vigil outside Diddi's door and wheezed his way painfully up the stairs and followed her like a dog. He was a shell of a man now, wizened and painfully thin, yet he cooked the most amazing meals when we reached Gulistan. Diddi had persuaded him to quit drinking some years ago and now he had the lost look that all reformed alcoholics have. One July, when Diddi was with me in Delhi recovering from a cataract operation, Kiran called up to say that Phainku was so ill that they had shifted him to the hospital. He had sent word that he wanted to see Diddi once before he died. Diddi immediately packed up her bags and left, brushing aside all my pleas that she should not travel so soon after her surgery. As soon as she reached Lucknow, she went straight to the hospital to see him. It was pouring and Diddi was soaked to the skin, but she went to Phainku's bedside. She held his hand and he opened his eyes, unable to speak because of the oxygen mask. He lifted her hands to his head and then moved his eyes to where Kiran was standing, as if to say, I am leaving my children in your care. Diddi told him, I'm here, Phainku, you won't die, but he shook his head. She had barely reached her flat when news came that he had died.

'I know he waited for me,' she told me on the phone. 'Now

I am truly alone.' It was as if her last link with Lucknow had snapped.

~

A Woman Called Ramrati

An obituary by Diddi (late 1980s):

'Once upon a time…' may be a clichéd way to begin a story but the most beloved tales have just such a beginning. Today, as I sit down to write a tribute to an illiterate but immensely wise woman, her happy, smiling face is right before me. Yet to speak of her in the past tense is as painful as performing her last rites. Believe me, the most difficult pen portraits are the ones that have the cleanest outlines. There is no distinguished ancestry, no brilliant academic record, no prominent names to drop, no noble bloodlines to trace: such a sketch has to be drawn without recourse to imagination or stylistic devices.

Ramrati was painfully thin and no matter how hard we tried to make her put on some flesh, the needle of the weighing machine never moved beyond 29 kilos. But what energy and zip she had! I used to wonder from where she got that bounce but then I could also never understand how such a pure and simple soul had survived the hardships of her life and remained so unfailingly cheerful and happy. When I hired her twenty-two years ago, my husband was not at all happy about the appointment. 'There are already too many helpers in this house. What's more, she works in other homes and may well spread their dirt across our threshold. I think our privacy is being invaded.'

'She's not like that at all,' I insisted, and Ramrati came into our lives. From the first day, she took over my home and life. Years later, when my husband was dying, he confessed, 'You were right about Ramrati: she will always stand by you.' I should have felt vindicated but his tone was that of a man who knew he would not live long and who was making sure that I would have a companion after he was gone. Ramrati took over the entire burden of my sorrows after he died. Although I had known for some time that my husband did not have much time, his death robbed me of my very sense of self. Nothing made sense any more and I could see no future that gave me hope. I had always believed in his honesty and admired it, but it meant now that there were no savings, not even an insurance policy to turn to. I tried to write but my pen, like some stubborn mule, refused to move across the sheet of paper in front of me. It was hopeless, nothing was going to work any more, I decided, so I called Ramrati and told her, 'Ramrati, I can't afford to keep you any more—find yourself another house to work in.' After her husband lost his job, I had taken over the care of her entire family: in my present state I felt such a burden was impossible to handle.

'Listen to her!' she told an unseen audience, her arms akimbo. 'Find yourself another job, she tells me! Am I a selfish cat, Diddi, that I will leave you now when the milk and cream have gone?'

So she stayed on. What is more, she refused to take a salary until I got some money from my husband's pension and gratuity. Mrinal was abroad those days, Ira had a young child and Micky was still at the IIT. My eldest daughter, Veena, stayed with me for three months but she had to join her husband in Hawaii and left as well. The day she left, Ramrati arrived at my flat, holding her bedding under her arm. 'Here I am, mahtari,' she announced cheerfully. 'This is where I will now stay.' She spread her bedding on the floor next to my bed and posted herself as my night attendant. She stood over me like a mother, watching every morsel I left uneaten, every drop of milk undrunk. If ever a sob escaped my lips, her sharp ears heard it immediately. 'Want to damage your eyes, now, do you? What do you think, Diddi, that your tears will bring back Saheb?' she asked.

One day, she handed me a pen and some paper. 'Here you are, now write,' she said brusquely. 'You know, Diddi,' she said in a gentler tone, 'when my uncle died in the prime of his youth, my grandmother used to sit up all night grinding wheat. I got up to help her once and she shooed me away. It isn't wheat that I grind, Ratiya, she told me. I'm grinding away my pain.'

That was the first time that I wrote something and never read it over. I sent the article ('*Bandheesh ne aar mayaar dore*') to *Navneet* and was flooded with letters from fans. I realized then how I had been given a lesson no one but an illiterate woman like Ramrati could have given me. Grinding the pen across paper did not merely lessen my pain, it helped me reach out to hundreds of fellow-sufferers.

Ramrati never ceased to amaze me with her wisdom. 'I have never hurt anyone in this life, Ramrati,' I said to her one day. 'Then why has God chosen to punish me so?'

She was silent for a while, still as a statue. Then, she said slowly, 'It is not for the wrongs done in this life that we suffer, Diddi. We pay the debts of the last life in this one. That tobacco that you chew all the time—all your children have told me, Make her give it up, Ramrati. Hide her box—tobacco causes cancer. Have I succeeded in doing what they say? You keep yelling at me for smoking bidis and burning my lungs. Have you succeeded in making me give it up? Arrey, these are all addictions we carry over from another life. Disease, land and property, lawsuits and cases, the noose, jails, addictions like yours and mine—all these are the interest we have to pay on our past karma.

We inherit our fate in this life from an earlier birth and pay for those mistakes now. He is a mean old usurer, that Old Man up there, Diddi. Until He has extracted every last paisa, He won't let you live in peace.'

I looked at her simple face in consternation—she had read no Veda or Upanishad, but what a complete understanding she had of what the profoundest Vedantic philosophers have said. Ramrati's simple homespun wisdom was based on a solid knowledge of the aphorisms of Ghagh and Bhaddari, old folk poets of rural India. If the sky was dark with black clouds and I looked for an umbrella before stepping out of the house, she would tell me, 'Why do you need an umbrella? Go, it won't rain—black clouds don't bring rain. It's the brown ones that pour.' Her personal met office never let her down. I used to eat a karela (bitter gourd) every day but did not dare to ask her for one in the month of Kuar. Ramrati was fond of saying *Kuar karela, Kartik dahi; maribo nahin to paribo sahi.* (Eat a karela in Kuar and curds in Kartik: then if you don't die, you will certainly fall ill.)

I have no one now to tell me what to do or eat. I come back in the burning heat of the afternoon and there is no Ramrati ready with chilled water in a shining glass, saying lovingly, 'Here, cool down first.' Lucknow is notorious for its sudden power cuts but as soon as the fan stopped whirring, there was Ramrati with a handfan that her frail wrists moved ceaselessly until the power came back. Of course, there was no point in telling her to stop.

When I came back from Delhi after receiving the Padma Shri, Ramrati greeted me with a garland of red roses. Then came a plate of laddoos that she lovingly stuffed into my mouth. God knows where she had scrounged the money to buy them. My eyes filled up: my own literary community had forgotten to congratulate me but this simple, unlettered woman had probably blown her weekly allowance to show me how happy my award had made her. A few weeks later, I developed a sudden, shooting pain in my right arm. I couldn't even hold a pen. *Dharmayug* had sent frantic telegrams to say they needed the next episode of my serial then being published. But try as I might, I couldn't lift pen to paper. 'I don't think I can write any more, Ramrati,' I told her.

'Nonsense,' she said briskly. 'I know what has happened— it's the evil eye that has cast its jealous spell on your success after the Padma Shri. I'll fix it this Sunday.'

That Sunday, I had some important visitors. 'Psst, Diddi,' she beckoned me from the door. 'Don't say anything, I'm taking off that nazar.' One hand held a plate of burning coals, the other had red chillies, lime and god knows what else. She waved all this seven times round my head and shoved the lot on to the burning coals. Acrid fumes from the burning chillies filled the house and my visitors nearly died coughing. 'Looks like something's burning in the kitchen,' spluttered one politely. I nodded weakly. How could I tell them that they had to suffer this for the sake of my painful arm?

What Ramrati loved above all to do was travel and bum around. She was just ten when she was married off. Had a step-mother-in-law and a hopeless alcoholic as a husband. Then came a string of girls—all this aged her before her time. She started working in people's homes, on construction sites as a daily labourer, sold headloads of grass—in short, did whatever she could to feed her family. In addition to all this was the daily thrashing she received from her husband. 'When my grandmother heard that Phalane [she never took her husband's name, so she called him Phalane, which means "that one"] treated me badly, she handed me a bundle of money and said,

Leave the man, Ratiya, and come back to me. We will find you someone else.'

'Don't you dare say this again,' Ramrati told her. 'He is my husband, he held my hand as I left this house, how can you ask me to leave him? He can leave me if he wants—I won't.' In this age, how many hands can claim to have such loyal holders, I wonder.

Often her husband would blow his entire salary in some hooch shop and come home on unsteady legs with empty pockets. Occasionally one would hear that he was lying drunk in some gutter. Whenever she heard that, Ramrati ran to find him, loaded him on to a rickshaw and washed his vomit-smeared clothes and face. Then she would quietly put a thali of food in front of him. In return, he would shower her with vile abuses and kick the food away. Sometimes, she would come sobbing to me: 'Diddi, Phalane is "dawn" again today. Someone flicked the money from his pocket and now he is cursing all my sisters and mother's family with words I can't even utter.'

'And this is the man you worship!' I exploded. 'Go, lick his feet.' I had actually seen her drink the water after she had washed his feet. Yet perhaps it was such wifely devotion that later turned Phalane into her devoted slave. He gave up drinking altogether and, in his old age, he showered her with all the love he should have given her in her youth. Ramrati took full advantage of this altered power structure. The minute she reached her quarter after finishing my work, she would begin ordering her husband around. 'Phalane, make my bed and get some cold water while you are at it. I want to stretch out a bit.' Then one day I saw she was doing her own work once more. 'What happened?' I asked. 'Why don't I hear you ordering your Phalane any more?'

'What to do, Diddi,' she replied. 'Ammaji [that is how she referred to my mother] was standing on the terrace the other

163

day and saw Phalane putting my petticoat to dry on the line. She was furious. How dare you sit around while your husband does the housework, she yelled from there. I swore then that I wouldn't make Phalane do my work any more.' But that did not stop her from throwing her weight around whenever she could. 'I know who has made you so bossy,' I heard him mutter one day, and I knew who he meant.

'I know, too,' she shot back. 'Just try and bully me again and see what Diddi will write in the papers about you.' How they worshipped me! Ramrati would follow me like a shadow but never once did her husband complain of her shameless neglect. I had snatched his wife away from him, but he never once objected. As a matter of fact, I would occasionally tell her, 'Ramrati, you stay here all day, even after your poor husband comes back tired from work. Go sit with him and cheer him up.'

'Why?' she retorted. Then she sighed. 'When we could have sat and laughed together he never as much as smiled my way. Now we have only nasty barbs to exchange.' Truly, they could not spend a pleasant moment together.

'Can't stand each other, but can't do without each other either: that is what the two of you are about. Why don't you at least keep your mouth shut, Ramrati?' I told her once.

'What is a dal without some tempering, Diddi? Unless a man and his wife exchange a nasty word or two, life together will be so bland.'

What a perfect critique of a happy marriage that was! 'Can you imagine constantly hanging round each other's neck?' she went on. 'I have been beaten black and blue by this man, Diddi, but that is also why he cares so much for me now.' And yet, for all the fireworks that flew between them, they were devoted to each other.

Her right wrist had a tattoo on it—a rose in a pot, Radha Krishna in a classic pose and on top of it all her husband's name: Phikkulal. With time, the purple colour of the tattoo became even richer and I wondered whether the darkening colour was an indication of their deepening love.

'What is it like to fly in a plane, Diddi?' she asked me one day.

'Have you ever sat in a carousel? Landing in a plane is a little like that,' I told her.

'Of course, I have,' she retorted. 'That's where I first saw Phalane.' And then she told me the story of their strange courtship. I wish I could write as graphically as she spoke. I may call myself a writer, but my Ramrati was a born storyteller. 'It was the Gudiya ka mela, Diddi,' she started. 'I must have been some ten years old or so. I insisted, as children do, on being taken there.'

Then came a description of her getting ready: 'I had bangles on my arms up to the elbows, a flowered sari with a wide border, a tikli on my forehead, kajal in my eyes, missi between my teeth to make them shine brighter, silver anklets and bells on my toes. I had a mouth stuffed with paan, and never realized for a moment that Phalane was in the chair just above mine and watching me.'

'Then?' I asked, hardly able to contain my curiosity at the development of the plot.

'The carousel started to move and then,' a dramatic pause here, 'Phalane dropped his scented handkerchief on me. I was livid! Who is this bastard who's dropped this on my lap, I thundered. May I dance at his funeral, God knows where this goon came from! My mother jabbed me and said, Keep your mouth shut, don't you know this is the man we are trying to get you married to? Then three days later, I went to the well to fill water and who do I see? Phalane, standing there twirling his

165

scented kerchief again! Hey there, you girl, he said. Get me some water to drink. Why, I flashed back. Am I your father's servant or something? Not yet, he said mysteriously, but one day you will be my slave. And then, Diddi, when the time came for that, he made me slave so hard that I can't even begin to tell you!'

Another passion of hers was going to the movies. Her favourite stars were Dharmendar and Amitabh Bachchan and she had named them Dharmendaruwa and Amitabhuwa. A few years ago, I had to go to Bombay. That was the time when Amitabh Bachchan was hanging between life and death and Ramrati was distracted with grief. She had been to every pir and temple to pray for him. 'Ai, Diddi,' she asked me. 'Will you meet Amitabhuwa there?'

'Why?' I asked.

'My Diddi,' she pleaded, 'just tell him, Bachuwa, Ramrati sends you her love.'

I couldn't help but laugh at this simple request. She had never seen the man and yet she wanted him to know she was as concerned as his mother. I did pass on her message to Amitabh. She was also a TV junkie in the worst sense of the word. From *Krishi Darshan* to the last transmission, she avidly watched every programme. And when the serial *Ramayan* was being telecast, her life came to a standstill. She would drop everything she was doing and sit at the dot of eight in front of the TV, red rose in hand, and prostrate herself before the serial started with a loud *Siyavar Ramchandra ki jai!* She had been completely floored by Ram's smile and once told me, 'You know, Diddi, there are just three people in the world who have that smile: *Ramayan*'s Ram, Rajiv Bhaiyya [Rajiv Gandhi], and our Radhika bitiya [my granddaughter].'

Whenever Rajiv Gandhi came to Lucknow, his cavalcade had

to pass in front of my house as that was the way to the airport. Ramrati would warn me early in the morning: 'I'm off to see Rajiv Bhaiyya, no work from me today.' Then, 'Diddi, which sari shall I wear?' as if Rajiv Bhaiyya was coming to Lucknow specially to see her sari. I was reminded of a lovely Tagore poem called 'Rajar Dulal':

> O ma! The prince is going to pass the road in front of our house this morning. Tell me, how can I possibly do any housework today? Tell me, ma, what shall I wear? How shall I braid my hair? Which jewels and sari shall I choose?
>
> Why are you looking at me like that, ma? I will stand in that corner where he won't even see me. It will be over in the blink of an eye and he will leave for some far-off land. But tell me, when the prince is going to pass our house, how can I not dress up to see him?

My Ramrati would stand in the sun for hours exactly as Tagore's character did to catch a glimpse of Rajiv Bhaiyya as he whizzed past her in a flash.

She travelled with me whenever it was possible for me to take her—I took her to Bombay, Banaras, Kanpur, Rewa, when the universities there called me for a lecture or to confer an honorary degree. Ramrati would pack a bundle of clothes and jump at the chance. 'Now remember, Ramrati,' I warned her, 'you are not allowed to smoke inside air-conditioned compartments. No smoking there, understand?' This was a huge punishment and, after a few hours of abstinence, I could sense her restlessness. God knows how hard I tried to make her give up smoking—hid her packet of bidis, yelled and screamed but to no avail.

When she could no longer control the urge to light up, she

would whisper pathetically, 'Ai mahtari, my jaw will fall off yawning if I don't go. Can I go to the loo and sneak a sutta?' 'Go then, I hope you die there!' I would curse and she would speed off.

Much against her wishes, I sent her daughters to school. One of them, Kiran, became the first girl to graduate in her community. Ramrati was hugely proud of this fact, but it worried her too. 'Where will I find a boy as educated as her in our community?' she would ask me.

Kiran was my favourite among her daughters: I had brought her up from the age of seven and Ramrati had declared that I would have to give her away when she married. And that is exactly what I did. Kiran's kanyadan was the fourth one I performed. The wedding took place in my house and with more fanfare than the weddings of my own three daughters. Halwais were called to make sweets, a shamiana sprang up and, on Ramrati's special request, revolving coloured lights lit up the facade of my flat. The barat arrived and I almost fainted when I saw the groom riding an elephant. Ramrati was so overawed by the spectacle when she went to perform the arti that her knees were knocking. Never in her wildest dreams had she imagined that an elephant would stand at her threshold. After we saw the barat off, she fell at my feet, her eyes streaming with tears of pure joy and gratitude. 'I have now completed all my duties, mahtari,' she said.

Sadly, she became frailer and frailer after that wedding. 'What is happening to the two of us, Ramrati?' I joked. 'We seem to take turns falling ill nowadays.'

A lovely smile lit up her gaunt face. 'Know what, Diddi? Both of us need overhauling—all the tubes and tyres need changing now.'

What I did not know then was that she would beat me to the

168

body shop. I had a premonition about her death for a while. When I returned to Lucknow after a long spell at my children's, she was a bag of bones confined to her bed. She looked like a little girl, a mere skeleton as she lay there. But her lovely smile still irradiated her face as she greeted me. 'My Diddi has come back. Nothing will happen to me now.'

She really believed that I could stall death and that as long as I was around she would not die. Twice I managed to snatch her back from the edge: once when she vomited blood and I rushed her in an ambulance to the hospital. The second time, when she had what I suspect was her first heart attack. 'Ai Diddi,' she called out to me. 'Save me, I'm scared.' I saved her once again. By the evening she perked up and told me, 'I know, mahtari, even that bastard Yama is scared of you...'

She was convinced that I could control Death and that Yama listened (as she thought everyone else did) to me. That is why when I had to go out of Lucknow on some unavoidable business, she began to weep like a child, 'Don't leave me, my mother. Mahtari, please stay!'

But I had to leave her, although I had already seen all the signs of her impending death. Water streamed continuously from her left eye, the lobes of her ears had turned the other way, the nose looked crooked and the hair on her head stood up like the quills of a porcupine. I knew then that my devoted companion would not be there when I returned. I sat near her, stroking her scrawny feet as she slept but the moment she awoke she pulled them away. 'Why are you pushing me to hell now, Diddi, please don't touch my feet...'

Finally, it was time to say goodbye. With great difficulty she clasped both my hands in her bony hands and lifted them to her head. I will never forget that look—a heart-melting picture of pathetic helplessness, tears streaming down her face. Unable to speak, we just gazed at each other for a long time.

My favourite witch doctor was being vanquished by Death and I watched helplessly. Her healing powers were well known all over the town. Several sick people came to her door to seek help: an infant's teething problems, a dislocated collarbone, hernia, blood dysentery, earache, toothaches—Ramrati could mend them all with herbs, potions or charms. As for fixing a strained back, she was blessed by birth to heal that problem. 'I was a breech baby,' she told me proudly. 'If I kick a strained back, there is no way the pain won't go.' However, the magic worked only on Sundays and Tuesdays. You should have seen the milling crowds outside her house on those days. They would come clutching their backs and Ramrati would give them a resounding kick. 'Go, run!' she would proclaim confidently. I have actually seen people bent double with pain depart smiling. One Sunday, she came in very late, perhaps there had been an unprecedented rush. 'This is getting too much, Ramrati.' I scolded her. 'At this rate, you will have to choose between your patients and my home.'

'Forgive me, Diddi,' she said, 'but a real upstart of a thanedar came today. Said, I hear you cure strained backs, will you be able to fix mine? Listen to him, I said. Hundreds have drowned here and a donkey asks if there is enough water? I have handled brigadiers and police inspectors. Who do you think you are? Go, stand there, I told him. Then gave him such a kick, Diddi, that I knocked the wind out of his guts!'

How could I say anything after that? However, my back was the only one she would not kick to fix, no matter how much I begged her to. She bit her tongue and touched her ears in horror. 'Ram-Ram! Don't ask me to do this, Diddi. I would rather die than hurt you.'

She loved my children more than she loved hers. She had

seen them grow up, marry and become mothers. She was my ambassador who took gifts and presents when my grandchildren were born and came back laden with gifts for herself. My youngest daughter had twin boys, who were dearer to her than all the other grandchildren. She spent a month looking after them in Faizabad and reported the experience to me in great detail. 'Know what, Diddi? I used to take the two angels in a pram and people would stop to ask whose babies they were. And I would tell them, who else can they be in Raja Ram's kingdom? These are Luv and Kus.'

Over the years, she had acquired a unique collection of English words that she loved to show off. Vice Chancellor became Vice Tantalur, *Blitz* was Blood Pressure according to her, Fanta became Elephanta and Gorbachev was Karva Chauth. Occasionally, her English proved more effective than ours. A certain pest had once taken to calling me at odd hours of the night. He would ask for Ramrati's daughters and make lewd comments about them, or tell me to stop writing else he would send terrorists to kill me. We were both fed up with the nightly intrusion. Then, Ramrati decided to take charge. 'This time, mahtari, don't pick up the foon when he rings. I'll take care of this terrorist myself.'

The phone rang at midnight. Ramrati picked it up and the conversation went something like this:

'Hellooo! Who is it?'

'Is Shivaniji there?'

'Yes, she is.'

'What is she doing?'

'Choosing the flowers to decorate your bier.'

He must have said something after that and Ramrati thundered, 'Yew bleddy basturr!'

She banged the phone down and turned to me triumphantly.

'I learnt that one from my father-in-law, mahtari. He was a khansama with the Angrez sahebs, was the old man. If that fool can understand English, he will keep his mouth shut after that!'

It worked: that fool never rang again.

Her simple faith was truly touching. I can never forget one particular incident. When I returned from Haridwar after performing my husband's last rites, my own house appeared strange and new. However hard I tried, I could not sleep at night. On one such night, oppressed by the heat of the summer and my heavy heart, I dragged a chair to the terrace and sat down. As silently as a cat Ramrati came and sat at my feet and put her head against my knees. 'You know, Diddi, when you were not here, saheb came every day...'

'What rubbish is this, Ramrati?'

'Believe me, Diddi, every evening he would come and sit at the threshold of your room.'

She explained then how a sparrow came every one of those ten days that I was away and sat at my doorstep, darting looks all round the room. He came alone, according to her, accompanied by no mate, no friend. 'When I lit the evening lamp and put it outside, I would fold my hands and tell him, Saheb, it is getting dark now. Perhaps it is time for you to leave. And he would quietly fly off.'

I could picture the scene: the sparrow at my doorstep and Ramrati, her face veiled modestly, both her hands folded reverently, telling the sparrow, 'Saheb, it is getting dark now. Perhaps it is time for you to leave.'

I could not laugh at her then, nor can I laugh now. I did ask then, 'So why does your saheb not come any more, Ramrati?'

'Why should he come now, Diddi? You set him free at Haridwar.'

After her daughters were married, she had to face the same

problems that all mothers of married daughters face: have to send gifts on the birth of a grandchild, on Karva Chauth, clothes today for a son-in-law, money to a daughter at some festival or other. Every day she came with some request for help. Occasionally, I would lash out. 'You are going to clean me out, Ramrati. Do I have a gold mine here? Why don't you ask someone else for help?'

Head bowed, she stood silently. Then, she said in a resigned tone, 'Where else can I go, mahtari?' I kick myself today for my harsh words and remember another poem from Tagore:

These hands spread before you seek

Not alms, but a giver...

In all her years with me she only asked for two favours: one, that I should give her daughter Kiran away when she married and two, that when it was time for her to go, I would make all the arrangements for her funeral. 'Phalane will never have money even for that! And I don't want to be covered in a shroud paid for by my daughters, Diddi!'

She was my soulmate and that is perhaps why I was able to honour both those promises. Her body had barely turned cold when my sister called me to tell me that Ramrati had died. And I immediately arranged money for her last journey. This year on my husband's death anniversary, I missed her the most. Each year, on this day, she would arrive at the crack of dawn, clean and sweep the doorstep of the house, anoint it with cowdung and reverently carry the food to be given to the cow. Once when my son was performing the ritual anniversary puja, I saw her wipe her eyes with her sari. 'What made you weep today?' I asked her later.

'As I was watched Bhaiyya perform the rites at the puja, the sacred thread shining on his bare shoulder, I realized that I have no son, Diddi. Who will do this for me when I am gone?'

'Why, you have daughters, don't you? Their sons…' 'Go on, Diddi…' she laughed. 'A son is a son. Want to know what I have to say about sons of daughters? A daughter's son is like a donkey's piss on the sand…it vanishes!'

And we both laughed merrily.

I can't laugh today. After my son was asked by the priest to remember all his ancestors and pray for them, he said finally, 'Now you can remember all your dear ones and pray for them as well.' It was at the tip of my tongue to say a prayer for her, no blood relative yet dearer to me than my own children. But dare I voice such heresy? The Hindu religion has a forbidding code of conduct and no one can subvert its laws. As a woman, I cannot play a part in any ritual relating to death. Nor can I place the sacred thread on my bare right shoulder and pray for the moksha of Ramrati's soul.

Yet this I will say for her: *Anadi nidhano Dev shankh chakra gadadhar, akshay pundareekasho prêt mokshaprada bhav.* (O Lord of the small and poor, you who hold the conch, the mace and the chakra, release her from the eternal cycle of birth and death and grant her soul moksha.)

10

The Last Chapter

Her life in Lucknow fulfilled Diddi in a way that I can now understand, for it gave her a strength she lost when she was in a boring, normal, domestic situation. Like a Samson shorn of his locks, Diddi lost her energy when surrounded by placid people. Unfortunately for her, we were all married into normal households where things ran smoothly and kitchens and store cupboards were neatly arranged. Ever since I can remember, Diddi generated noise and excitement wherever she was and in whatever she did. When she went into the kitchen, she had to have at least two people in attendance to fetch and run for her and she banged lids, cursed bottles that she could not open and yelled when she could not find a ladle or spoon or whatever. Minu used to say that if Diddi ever stubbed her toe, she slapped the first child she met. But at the end of this drama, she produced delicious, finger-licking food although the kitchen looked as if a tornado had swept through it. She always left the debris to be cleared by those who put store by neatness and orderliness: her job was to create the meal.

In Lucknow, installed in her lively court, she was surrounded by those who looked upon her as their saviour and this encouraged her to become more and more eccentric as she grew older. She was the source of the strength and succour of her staff—outside Lucknow, she felt this identity was erased and she became an appendage to the lives of her children. Nothing was more difficult for her to accept than this secondary status: she was accustomed to being the centre of her universe, so to become a mere satellite in other lives was an unacceptable alternative. She would have dearly loved for us to visit Lucknow regularly but when we started to visit her less and less, she accepted that it was time to let us go. So although her life in the last decade or so was lonely beyond compare, it was a solitary imprisonment that, like Ama, she chose to inflict on herself.

Then one day, in April 1997, while she was alone in Lucknow, she went to the bathroom at three in the morning and vomited blood. Being Diddi, she did not wake up Kiran, Ramrati's daughter, who always slept near her bed. She waited till the morning to tell her so as not to alarm anyone. Kiran rang me up at six in the morning, sobbing into the phone. 'Come now!' she wept.

I called the others and all of us rushed to book ourselves on whatever was going to Lucknow—plane, train or taxi. By this time, Diddi had been rushed to the hospital by her neighbours and Anil, the doctor who lived a few flats away, gave her a Vit K injection to stem the haemorrhaging. Then he took her personally over to the hospital and stayed until my brother reached a few hours later. The diagnosis numbed us: Diddi had cirrhosis of the liver and she was bleeding from a ruptured blood vessel.

The next few days were a nightmare. I lost count of how many times she was rushed to the ICU as she bled from a fresh source. Fifteen days later we were still in the hospital and Diddi had become as weak as a kitten. It was imperative to take her to Delhi as none of us could stay on in Lucknow much longer and the doctors warned us of dangerous infections that she may pick up from the hospital the longer she stayed there. Twice we booked ourselves on a plane to Delhi and each time a fresh crisis erupted and the tickets had to be cancelled.

Diddi's illness was reported widely in the local papers and the Governor of Uttar Pradesh, Motilal Vora, sent his secretary to us one day offering us the state plane to fly her out to Delhi. So we reached Delhi in the Uttar Pradesh state plane and drove her straight from the airport to AIIMS, Delhi's premier medical institute. Among the doctors who treated her were many who had read her works and, all day, doctors and nurses would troop into the room to ask for her autograph. Their care ensured that she recovered and she was told she had been granted a fresh lease of life. However, we were warned that she must get herself checked every month so that the doctors could investigate if any fresh bleed was imminent and take remedial measures. I think this was the first time I saw her submit meekly to us and she spent the next six months in Delhi, moving from one child's house to another's. When she realized that she was better, she began to fret about leaving Lucknow for so long. 'I am fine,' she told us and bullied the doctors until they allowed her to return once more to her lair.

For the next seven years, she fooled us all into believing that she had made a complete recovery. And indeed, although she was a frailer, much reduced shadow of her former self, she did not stop writing or travelling. She went to Boston, where my brother had gone in 1999, to see his new house and to London to deliver a lecture at a World Hindi Conference. She was above seventy by now, yet she travelled alone, braving a journey that would intimidate most people of her age, leave alone someone who was as ill as she was by then. Diddi's younger sister Indira and her doctor husband had migrated to Washington several years ago and Diddi spent many weeks with them. My aunt Indira's sons and daughters-in-law were well-known doctors and one of them taught at the prestigious Johns Hopkins Hospital. They offered to get her checked by the best doctors in the US. 'Do you know,' Diddi told me on her return, 'the doctor who checked me called his students to show them a woman of seventy-five who had all her own teeth and perfect blood pressure. I told you that you panic unnecessarily: I will live to be eighty.'

Diddi almost made it to eighty. Then, in April 2001, she was violently ill again. This time, she had acute acitis—fluid had bloated her stomach as her liver withered and she could hardly breathe. All that could be done now was a periodic draining of the stomach cavity. The doctors would insert a long needle to aspirate the fluid from her abdomen but, because her liver was slowly failing, it would fill up again in a few weeks. It was a painful procedure but Diddi bore it without a murmur. She would lie there in the hospital bed, a huge vat on the floor collecting the fluid drained from her body and calmly read a book through the entire procedure! All around her were moaning patients. Some she wrote about, and around some she created funny anecdotes to regale us with. But her eyes told a different tale. They were full of a knowledge she tried to hide from everyone: that she was living on borrowed time.

That August, she went to Boston once again, and met all her grandchildren who were by now either studying or working there. She called my niece Radhika, Mrinal's daughter, so that she could bless her first great-grandchild, Arnaaz, and my brother organized a party for her birthday in October with all the grandchildren there. She returned in late October and after a few weeks with Mrinal in Delhi flew off to Lucknow, despite all our pleading. She looked fine to us and we gave in once more. She sounded tired on the phone whenever I called her but brushed off all requests to come to Delhi fast.

She had hardly been there three weeks, when Kiran called me one day. 'Iru Diddi,' she said in a low voice so that Diddi could not hear from her room, 'she is really bad now. *Hamko dar lag raha hai*, I am scared, what shall I do? Yesterday Diddi and I went to the hospital and—'

'How did you go?' I interrupted, knowing that my mother had no car and the hospital was a good hour's drive from her flat.

'Diddi called a taxi and she insisted on walking down that long corridor to reach the doctor's chambers. He took one look at her and said, Shivaniji, either you get into hospital now or else go to Delhi immediately. So,' Kiran quickly told me, 'I have rung up Bhaiyya's office and they are sending a ticket across— she will be with you tomorrow.'

I had just taken up a new job—and my publisher wanted me to go to Calcutta to attend the book fair to launch a book there. It had involved days of setting up press interviews, appointments with authors there and, besides, how could I possibly tell him that a week after I had joined I wanted out? My plane took off from Palam airport as hers flew in. Mrinal and my husband were at the airport to take her straight to hospital, where her doctor had been informed she was coming in a very distressed state. But when things go wrong, nothing goes your way. On the way from the airport, their car was stuck in a traffic jam for an hour or so; my husband tells me she could barely sit—there was so much fluid in her body that she found it difficult to hold herself upright. She had asked to come to my house but obviously the hospital was where she had to be taken first. She asked where I was, because if I had told her that I was going to Calcutta, she would have checked into the Lucknow hospital and not come to Delhi at all.

I was shocked to see how frail she had become even in the three weeks that she had been in Lucknow. Her face was grey with exhaustion and she could hardly walk or even stand for more than a few minutes. 'I have come to your house to die,' Diddi said by way of a greeting, echoing the exact words that Ama had said to her when she came to Diddi all those years ago to spend her last months. Both of them had a very clear premonition of their impending death and knew that their time was up. Diddi used to say that Ama had even predicted that she would die on 18 March. By a strange coincidence, Diddi was to die on 21 March.

So this is why she had insisted on going back to Lucknow, I realized. She had gone there to say a final goodbye to her home and settle her bank and tax matters there. She told me the name of her bank manager who had promised to help out with the formalities when the time came. 'Why are you telling me all this?' I asked her angrily. 'You will be fine. Haven't we pulled you out of every crisis so far? Don't be dramatic.'

'This is the end,' she replied quietly. 'When I can face it, so can you. Now listen carefully: this is my will, these are my bank papers and Kiran knows all about my contracts and publishing details.' She handed me a file, turned her back and marched to her room.

This time, the acitis had gone beyond the stage where a periodic draining of the fluid in her body would work. Diddi's lungs were now filling up as well and her kidneys were failing. It was hopeless: just as the doctors dealt with one problem, another organ would signal distress. Every morning I got up with a sick feeling in my stomach: was today going to be her last? Finally, I called my brother in Boston and he flew down immediately. This, I knew, is what Diddi had always wanted. She told me, in her inimitable fashion, that if she ever died and he was not present, I was to put her body in a freezer until he came. She could not bear anyone else but her son to light her pyre. Binu came from Dehradun and Diddi said wryly to us one day that at last she had all her children next to her. 'It took a crisis like this to get you all here—if I had known, I would have offered to die years ago,' she joked.

What she could not bear, Diddi turned into a joke. These were sometimes off-colour and sounded very inappropriate. But there was no stopping Diddi—often she was criticized by our relatives for this and it hurt her deeply that they could not see what was so apparent to her and some of us. That life was a huge joke played on us—making sense of it would only make one mad. I remembered the time when both her eyes developed cataract simultaneously and she could barely see. She refused to acknowledge that it had started to become dangerous for her to continue staying alone and refused all offers of help to get her eyes checked up in Delhi. By now, it frightened her to spend so much time out of her lair in Lucknow, and then there was the question of finances. She was too proud to take help from any of the children. So she continued to go for her morning walks with Kiran shadowing her anxiously. Diddi laughed as she told me that she had once folded her hands in greeting to a tree because she thought it was someone she knew. Both of us laughed at the spectacle this must have presented to a passer-by.

One day, Binu called up and said, 'Please take her to Delhi and get her cataracts removed: she is virtually blind and I'm scared she is going to hurt herself one day.' The next day, Kiran called me up while Diddi was bathing so that she would not hear: 'Iru Diddi, I am afraid she is going to get hurt one day, she is walking into furniture and may stumble on the road.' With great difficulty I persuaded her to come and accept Micky's help in the expenses of the operation. While taking her to the hospital, I automatically held her hand as we climbed the stairs; she rudely shook me off. 'I'm not blind,' she barked and promptly stumbled. That night, as we lay in the peaceful private ward, both of us were worried: she about her surgery, I about the fact that I had a house full of guests, the twins had their final exams coming up and all my staff were on leave. 'Iru,' she called out. 'I'll pay you for the operation, why don't you get your eyes done, too? Think of the break you could take,' and we burst out laughing. Something she hated was pity: to her it was a great admission of failure.

And now, in her final days, she was determined to go down with the mask in place. Her jokes were a ploy to keep us from becoming sentimental and weepy—something she hated—as much as they were a wish to go when all of us were laughing together. She spent time with each one of us alone, and together. And all the while when we joked, or remembered the old days, we could hear the hours that were ticking away. 'You will be fine,' her doctor told her one day. 'I just had a patient who was over ninety and he went smiling from here.'

Diddi smiled at him. 'I am prepared to die, doctor,' she replied. 'I have had a good life—I have four wonderful children and I am so proud of what they have achieved. I have eight grandchildren and have seen and played with my great-grandchild. I have lived life on my terms and will pay for my own funeral. Why should I want anything more?'

Sadly, her body could no longer carry on: first her liver, then lungs and finally her kidneys started to give way. She had to be moved to the Intensive Care Unit and was taken away from a private room. For almost a week, she was kept there, unaware of the time or whether it was day or night. Worse, all around her were people in terminal conditions and, in fact, at least five people died in the week she was there. Her mind, sharp and alert to the end, registered all this and she no longer asked me restlessly when she was going to be released from the hospital.

It was no longer possible for us to ignore the truth: Diddi had just a few more days left. She must have seen our sorrow when we were allowed to visit her for a few minutes at a time, and that snapped her out of her own depression. One day, while she was still in the ICU, she told me, 'I know why I'm not getting better. The person in front of me is ugly as sin—if he were at least worth looking at, I might have tried getting better. As for my neighbour in the next bed...' At this point, I looked furtively at the comatose patient in the next bed, tied to tubes and instruments, his stentorian breathing through a ventilator shaking the bed. 'That one?' I asked. She nodded, 'All of last night he kept singing *Chalo man Kanpur ke teere, Kanpur ke teere...* First, he can't sing to save his life, he was disgustingly off-key throughout, and then,' she smiled at me, 'he got on my nerves. Finally, when I could take it no more, I pulled off my oxygen mask and said, Bhai sahib, drop me off at Lucknow on the way there.'

We both laughed and a passing nurse smiled—Diddi could not bear to see long faces around her and so to the end she kept the nurses and us amused with jokes and risqué comments about other patients. The nurses came to her for a break. 'Shivaniji, today your Keshto,' (another patient who had alcoholic cirrhosis and she had named Keshto after the famous actor who played drunks to perfection in Hindi movies), they would tell her, 'is making all of us really run.'

'Hasn't he died yet?' she asked them, quite aware that she herself had cirrhosis and would very soon probably be in the same hepatic coma he was in.

I have seen many die but no one went like Diddi. She had slipped into a coma in the last few days and I hope she was spared the pain that her body registered as one organ after another shut down. Her vital organs had collapsed: all that beat steadily to the end was her extraordinary heart. When it became apparent that nothing would save her now, we decided to pull out all the tubes and leave her with just the ones that fed her vital fluids. We also insisted she be moved out of the ICU and brought back into her room. All of us were there: all her children and their spouses and Kiran, her faithful shadow. I do not know whether she could hear us but we said all her favourite prayers and transmitted all our love. We were all standing around when the end came, looking at the monitor that showed her pulse slowly winding down. I saw a tear trickle from her left eye and then a flutter on her breast as the last heartbeat signalled the end. And she was gone. It was just getting on to five in the morning of 21 March.

She had always said that she would go at the Brahma Muhurta. This is that magical hour before dawn when the gods take all souls straight to their bosom, she used to say. As we returned from the hospital, a balmy spring breeze was blowing and I swear I felt her last caress on my cheek as she went to their bosom. The town was stirring into life: the azaan was calling the faithful to the mosque, shabads floated out of the nearby gurdwara and temple bells were ringing.

It was exactly the kind of closing chapter that my mother, with her strong preference for dramatic endings when writing her books, would have scripted.

~
_____

Epilogue: Pootonwali

This is among the last long stories Diddi wrote. It appears to me an
epitaph she wrote on her generation of parents.

He went through Chutke's letter once more, then neatly
folded it and hid it under the newspaper. If Parvati's eyes
spotted it she'd drive him mad with her questions: What has he
written? When does he want us to go across?

How was he going to tell her, 'Parvati, your Chutke has not
given the slenderest hint of when he wants us to come.' He had
already written thrice to Chutke that his mother was not well at
all, and that she had actually fainted a couple of times while
working. You know, he'd written, that your mother's eyes are
getting clouded over—one has glaucoma and the other a cataract.
The doctors have warned her that if she doesn't get them seen
to in time, she might lose her eyesight altogether. I don't have
to tell you what this village is like for medical help: there is a
hospital but no doctors. If you could arrange to get her seen by
a proper doctor, it would give me a lot of relief…

His clever son, however, had gauged his father's intentions,
so his reply was full of his own woes. I am due to be transferred
this April, he wrote back. I've spent five years here and they

have become very strict about extending tenures in Delhi, so I must return to my parent cadre. I am in such a fix, Babuji: Sujata is in her final year at school and Ronnie has just got admission in a new school with great difficulty. Sheila will also have to quit her job, else I'll have to leave the family behind in Delhi and carry on alone. But that means running two establishments...

So he had made it quite clear that, given his own troubles, a mother turning blind for lack of attention and a worried father were very low down on his list of priorities. Parvati came in quietly and put his cup of tea near him. 'I am sure,' she said in her soft voice, 'that we will hear from Chutke today.'

'To hell with Chutke and his letters,' he growled at her and watched her flinch. Instantly he regretted snapping at her: she'd become so frail, so slight that he was reminded of the cruel game he played as a schoolboy, when he loved to poke an earthworm with a stick. At the first jab of his stick, the creature would curl up into a little ball to protect itself from further torture. Parvati's pale face and stricken eyes reminded him of that cruel childhood pastime. Shame on me, he thought, what pleasure does one get from torturing the tortured? What joy have you ever been able to give her, his conscience smote him. In these forty-five years have you even put a drawstring in your pyjamas by yourself? Did you ever sew a button on to a shirt? What did you ever do for this woman who uncomplainingly brought up your family of five ungrateful sons? All she could ever afford to wear were the cheapest saris and petticoats but did she ever complain? Has any one of you ever given her even a plain gold ring to wear? If her father had not given her those twenty tolas of gold when she got married, would you have been able to bring up your family? Three of the daughters-in-law were given their ornaments from that hoard (the other two were given nothing because they were brought into the family by the sons without consulting him).

Parvati's father had been forced to keep that gold aside for his daughter because he realized that without that added allure his plain daughter may remain unmarried. She was illiterate, unremarkable in face and feature and so short that she could be mistaken for a dwarf. Added to this, she was timid beyond belief, a result of her mother's early death. Her father was the headmaster of the village school and had indeed sent her to school but she was so dumb that she failed three years running in the first class itself. In the meantime, her father remarried and Parvati drew further into her shell when she confronted her mean-eyed stepmother. Like a mesmerized rabbit when her stepmother was around, she ended up botching even the simplest task assigned to her. When she cooked, the vegetables would either be swimming in salt because she had added it twice or the rice was hard and inedible because she had drained too much starch and half the rice with it as well. Her trembling hands spilt the oil and milk with alarming frequency. Her stepmother screamed at her and Parvati wilted under the streaming abuses from her mouth, while her father stood like an impassive tree near a turbulent stream. Every year, Parvati's stepmother produced a new son and her father, overwhelmed by gratitude for this rich crop, became like putty in her evil hands. His mind, warped by the stepmother's lies and tales, made him blind to his daughter's misery and soon, encouraged by his new wife, he took to thrashing Parvati regularly. Ultimately, relief from this miserable life came when Parvati's father's sister found her a suitable boy.

'They are asking for a lot,' she told her brother, 'but then you won't easily get another boy like him.' And she was right: the boy was tall, handsome and well educated. Parvati's father decided that a generous dowry may wipe the cruelty he had heaped on his motherless daughter and quickly agreed to all the demands the boy's father made.

Shivsagar Mishra had passed out of the Kashi Vidyapeeth and just joined his first job. When he went home that year, his mother informed him that his father had chosen a bride for him: the daughter of one Harmendra Shastri of Faizabad. He lay awake that night wondering about his future bride. They had told him she was pink and white and he remembered meeting her father once, a handsome man with sharp features. So the daughter must be pretty, he deduced dreamily. The romantic lines of Kiratarjuna's Sanskrit verses came to his mind: 'Manini, my love, still your lovely hands that tremble like leaves / Else the bees that hover here, may fly away… Are these your eyes or the petals of a lotus? / Your eyelashes appear like a swarm of bees covering them… Is this your smiling face or the fragrant bloom of a royal lotus?…'

Shivsagar created a heroine in his mind and fell in love with her. Their marriage would be like the divine coming together of Shiv and Parvati, he dreamt on, and he would strut like a proud peacock as she followed him coyly when they returned with the marriage procession. He would lift her veil gently and be dazzled by what lay behind it…

But the truth was far from this dream: his Parvati sat on the bridal bed as gracefully as a dhobi's bundle. And when, after an inordinately long wait through the never-ending wedding rituals, he finally lifted her veil, his romantic fantasies stopped performing cartwheels in his head. His bride barely reached his knees and her blank gaze reminded him of a dumb mule. He could not find one feature in her that would inspire him to remember the lyrical conceits of Kiratarjuna's verses. Slowly, he learnt to live with the compromises his romantic soul was forced to make. His stern father would never understand his frustration even if he ever dared to voice it, and his mother was so delighted with the submissive Parvati that there was no point even reproaching her for saddling him with such a bovine wife. Parvati's dowry of twenty tolas of gold, the cows and buffaloes that she brought along with her and her humble, submissive nature were all Shivsagar's mother had ever wanted in a daughter-in-law. To add to her joy, Parvati produced five strapping sons in the next seven years. She never asked to visit her father's home nor did she ever fall ill. Above all, she appeared unfazed by her husband's deliberate indifference and followed him dutifully like a shadow.

When her youngest son, Chutke, was three years old, her father-in-law passed away. Yet, even after both his parents had died, Parvati refused to give up the veil and always covered her face modestly. Shivsagar was now the headmaster of the school and his house had a radio and two steel almirahs. He had also built three rooms on the first floor. Their sons were called Akhil, Amit, Ajay, Anil and Aditya—their far-sighted father had carefully chosen these names so that he would never have to look too far for the results of any competition to search for them. The boys did brilliantly in school and Parvati was often congratulated by the older village women on her good fortune. You are a true pootonwali, Parvati, they'd say, a blessed mother of sons. The boys were so good-looking that Parvati waved chillies and coals over their heads every Sunday and Tuesday to avert the evil eye. They grew up and, one by one, they all flew away to study. And Shivsagar and she were left all alone in their village.

They had lived together now for forty years and the placid tenor of their life had hardly rippled with change. Shivsagar was a little deaf but even now there was not a single strand of grey in Parvati's hair. She still woke at four in the morning, bathed and brought him his tea at his bedside. A little later, she dragged a chair in the sun and placed next to it a glass of milk, a bowl with five almonds, the newspaper and his spectacles. Then she went into the kitchen and started cooking. Over the years, perhaps out of years of practice, she had evolved into a superb cook and her food—whether a plain khichri or the elaborate meva ki gujiya—were renowned all over the village. 'Aji, there is no one who can cook like her anywhere in the village,' her mother-in-law boasted. Once, stung by his father's paeans of praise in honour of his wife's culinary skills, Shivsagar had commented sarcastically, 'You know, Babuji, a friend of mine says that the uglier a woman, the better her cooking.' His father had roared with laughter, for he thought his son was trying to provoke his bride but after that day, Parvati's veil came down a notch lower. Shivsagar could see that she was weeping behind it and was irritated at the thought of how ugly she looked when her nose turned red after a howl. He never forgave his father to the end for tying him down to such a cow.

Although Shivsagar refused to speak to his wife, Parvati never confided her misery to anyone in his family. So what if he never spoke to her—hadn't he given her five handsome sons? Would anyone believe her if she told them that her husband spoke directly to her for the first time after ten years of being married? He came to her only to satisfy the hunger in his loins but that day, when he went to the kitchen and found nothing to eat, he went furiously in search of her and found Parvati lying in her room, burning with fever. No doubt the boys had polished off whatever they found in the kitchen when they came home in the afternoon, for every jar was empty.

Searing loo winds raged outside, else he would have gone to the local halwai's shop. So Shivsagar stood at the threshold of

190

her room and yelled, 'Parvati, is there nothing to eat today? I haven't had anything to eat since the morning.' Parvati sat up quickly and even through the haze of her fevered brain, her husband's furious voice sounded to her like the sweet peal of temple bells. 'Did you say something to me?' she asked him softly, her eyes fixed on him as innocently as the clear gaze of a frightened faun. She could not believe that her husband, who had never so much as glanced her way and whose touch was a furtive, angry fumble on an occasional night of passion, would call out her name. She preened herself like a peacock and a joyous anticipation lit her face. 'Who else would I be talking to?' Shivsagar muttered ungraciously. 'I am starving.'

So far the only hunger that she had ever known him capable of was the stirring of his loins, but today he reminded her of one of her sons who said, 'Amma, give me something to eat. I am starving!'

She threw the sheet aside and made her way to the kitchen. Her head was throbbing with pain and her eyes were burning, yet she dished up hot puris and a delicious potato curry in record time even though her hands were trembling. She set the food on a thali and placed it before him. Within minutes, he had polished off a mound of puris, drunk a chilled glass of water and left for the school. Parvati could not lie down after that and that evening she made a meal fit for the gods to make up for keeping him hungry that morning. When the sons came home, they fell upon the food like an army of termites and licked their platters clean. Chutke asked her, 'What is so special today, Amma?' and she had no answer. Would the innocent child even understand what she was celebrating if she were to tell him, 'After ten years of being married to him, your father spoke to me for the first time today.' In any case, the boys were so full of their own news that no one waited for an answer.

The boys made their way out of the kitchen noisily, but there was no sign of their father. Night had fallen and the boys were fast asleep—Parvati was burning with fever again but waited patiently for her husband to eat her own meal. Shivsagar came finally and Parvati got up and went out with a lota of water for him to wash his hands in the courtyard. Silence. She took his thali, set out with the special meal and placed it on his usual table. Then she hesitated, almost expecting him to say, 'Go, Parvati, get your thali here as well. We'll eat together.' But there was not a word from Shivsagar. Then she heard Chutke talking to himself in his sleep and Parvati went slowly to her room to spend another lonely night. And the pootonwali, the blessed mother of five sons, curled her body into a small bundle as she carved out a place between her sleeping sons and prepared herself to be flailed by their thrashing limbs all night.

For years she had slept on this hard wooden takht with her sons, while Shivsagar slept in another room. If the sons were awake when she reached the room after locking up the kitchen for the night, a war would erupt for the privilege of sleeping next to her that night. And each time, Chutke would claim that place as his birthright and wrap his thin arms round her soft stomach so hard that she felt her intestines would pop out. Parvati had accepted her lonely life without a murmur, but that night she wept silently, feeling as if someone had snatched away a jug of water after offering her a drink. The tears continued to fall and soon turned into hiccups. She quickly stuffed her sari into her mouth in case she woke Chutke. What would she say to him if he asked her, 'Amma, why are you crying?'

She had long suspected that he wasn't unaware of his parents' relationship and one day, when they grew up, the boys were bound to find out. By the time they left their childhood behind them, they all knew that Babuji never spoke to Amma and yet their respect for their father remained undimmed. They hero-worshipped their tall, good-looking father and one roar from him turned them into submissive lambs. When the five boys sat with their father to do their sandhya in the puja room, Parvati's chest swelled with pride at the spectacle her handsome family presented. They say that a mother loves all her children equally but the truth is that every mother is especially partial to the weakest in her brood. Her Chutke was Parvati's favourite—a sickly child in his infancy, he was also the sweetest looking, his effeminate looks and innocent smile remained unblemished by puberty. The other boys had four sounds come simultaneously when their voice broke, but Chutke's voice, even when he became a man, always retained its sweet, flute-like pitch. His eyes filled up if anyone raised their voice at him, yet he was ahead of all the rest in class. Truly, all Parvati's sons were extraordinarily bright and, as they grew older, she began to believe the village women when they said she was a pootonwali—a blessed mother of sons.

'What a lucky man you are, brother,' Shivsagar's inseparable mate, Badri, used to say. 'Still a few years for you to retire and here you are, like a tiger who has polished off a kill and is now sitting on a boulder, licking his satisfied chops. Look at me! The light of my life earns four thousand, I'm told, but do you think he ever sends me a penny? I hear he is off abroad now. Says he'll return one day but take it from me, brother, an arrow and a son who goes abroad never return!'

Badri was not wrong. Shivsagar's elder son, Akhil, had been gone for seven years this summer—and did he return? He came once but how could he stay in a village now, after all the comforts he was accustomed to? They say that there they even have a gadget for sweeping the floors! He spent some time with one brother, some with another, some at his wife's parents'—with

193

all those who lived in cities. What had his father's mud-plastered village home to attract him there?

'See this, Babuji?' he'd shown him a gadget. 'This is an electric shaver. I'd show you how it works but there is no electricity in your village.' Shivsagar nearly said, 'Do you remember the time when all of you were taken to the village barber who was instructed to cut the hair so short that you would not have to come there for another month? And the barber's fee? An anna and a half!'

He'd brought a wristwatch for his father, along with a few bars of soap and some blades. For his mother there was a huge shapeless pullover that could have covered three women like her. Those gifts were still lying unwrapped in a tin trunk. He'd come for a day, and alone. The children had been left abroad— 'It's too expensive to buy tickets for everyone, Amma,' he explained to his mother. 'Let me earn a little more, and I'll bring them.'

They were still waiting for that day. Shivsagar sighed as he remembered ominous signs he'd noticed in their first-born in his childhood. Every morning, Shivsagar would make the boys write compositions to improve their language and vocabulary. Akhil would slyly cheat from his brothers and produce his work triumphantly. When someone called Justice Mishra came with a proposal for Akhil offering his daughter's hand, Shivsagar thought he was dreaming. Poor Shivsagar trembled with fear at the thought of welcoming a daughter-in-law whose father was a judge of the high court. He never realized then that it wasn't his humble home that had attracted the big man's notice but the brilliant son he had produced. So where was the question of the judge's daughter staying with her parents-in-law? She unrolled a magic carpet and both the son and his wife flew far away to another land.

Amit was the second son. Shivsagar had pawned Parvati's gold and jewellery to scrape together the fees for Amit when he qualified for the IIT. The day Amit passed out of the IIT, Justice Mishra swooped like an eagle and before Shivsagar had realized it, he snatched his second son away as well. Gita and Rita, the two Mishra sisters, had decided long ago that they would live abroad and that is where they were now, with Shivsagar's sons. The third son qualified for the civil services and Shivsagar's ears were deafened by the clamour of the dowry that was offered. Lakhs of money, a flat, a car and god knows what. Before Shivsagar could even consider the mountain of letters before him, his son settled the issue for him. He had been allotted the Tamil Nadu cadre and his first posting was in a remote subdivision. Jaundice struck him within a few days and he refused to inform his parents of his illness. Perhaps if he had warned them, he would have been saved. He admitted himself into the local hospital and fell in love with the Malayali nurse who looked after him. Shivsagar almost died of shock when he received a telegram that informed him of his son's marriage to an unknown girl from Kerala.

'You are dead for me,' Shivsagar wrote back. 'I forbid you to attend our cremation. Don't ever show me your face again.' He marched furiously to the postbox to mail the letter himself, his nostrils pinched with anger. Then he spat at the box and marched home. That was when he turned to Parvati for comfort—he no longer had the energy to bear his woes alone.

She saw him tearing the offending telegram and, taking in her husband's furious face, asked anxiously, 'What does it say? Is all well? No bad news I hope?'

'Yes,' he yelled back. 'It is terrible news. Amit is dead!'

'Hé Ram, Hé Ram,' said Parvati and fainted dead away, exactly as a leech melts when you sprinkle salt on it. 'Parvati! Parvati!'

he called out as he bent over her motionless body. Her pupils had retreated into her eyelids when he lifted them and her face was bloodless. Shivsagar panicked—Parvati's body was stone cold. O God, had she died of heart failure? If she left him at this age, who would take care of him? All his life he had kicked her away as if she was a mangy dog but faced with the prospect of a lonely life without her soothing presence, he lost his head completely. Not that his contrition did not have a touch of selfishness, for he knew that if he lost her no one would even throw a chapatti at him. Not one of his five sons was worth leaning on, except perhaps Chutke. He picked her up and put her inert body on the bed, rubbed her hands and feet vigorously but Parvati did not stir.

When nothing seemed to work, he ran to his friend Badri's house to fetch him. Badri had never been able to forgive his stone-hearted friend for humiliating his wife, yet the two had remained friends from school onwards, despite their different opinions on everything. Shivsagar would never swear or curse, not even in anger. Badri, on the other hand, began and ended each sentence with colourful abuses. He carried no burden on his shoulders—his only son had abandoned him and his wife had died many years ago. Badri ate and lived as he pleased—he drank, smoked and ate meat with no guilt. He accompanied Shivsagar every Tuesday to the local Hanuman temple but scrupulously avoided going in. 'Fat and free,' he was fond of saying, 'I live as I please.' For seventy years this was his mantra— he cared neither about the past nor worried about his future. After he broke off with his son, he never kept in touch with him and lived on his small pension. If he ever needed help, he went to his friend, Shibu.

'What's happened? Tell me the truth, bastard,' Badri said when he saw Shivsagar and ran to his house with him. Shivsagar fell on his wife's inert body and began to sob like a child. 'Forgive me, Parvati,' he cried. 'I have really tortured you. I am a butcher, Parvati, a butcher,' he sobbed. Badri watched his taciturn friend for a while and then said briskly, 'A butcher you may have been, idiot, but what is past is past. Here, help me lift her body to the floor. Go fetch some Gangajal and some kush.' The two heaved Parvati's body to the floor and then, to Badri's utter surprise, Shivsagar fell on his wife's body and began to kiss it madly— her bloodless lips, her temples, hair, forehead and feet.

'Have you gone mad?' Badri asked him. 'You will hurt her spirit if you go on like this!' and shook his friend's shoulder. 'Sit here quietly while I go and inform the others. We'll have to take her to the ghat soon and it's going to pour any minute from the look of those clouds outside.' Then he glanced at Parvati's body one last time and said wonderingly, 'Look! Look! She is breathing! Hai Ram, we were going to commit a hideous crime just now, Shibu! In fact, I was just wondering how a sati-lakshmi like her could have died on such an inauspicious day— today is Amavasya, the moonless night. Look, Shibu, just keep this between us, all right? Don't ever breathe a word of this to anyone, not even to your wife, understand? She will never forgive us. I'll quickly go home and fetch some malti-basant my father left me and we'll give it to her with some hot milk. Bappa used to say, Badri, even a corpse on his pyre will rise if you put a few drops of my malti-basant in his mouth!'

They gave her the magic potion and sat vigil over her all night. Shivsagar did not even bat an eyelid and, slowly, Parvati's breathing became stronger and more regular. Badri turned to his friend and slapped his back. 'Go, salé, make some strong tea for us. The cold has frozen my ribs, I swear. Don't worry, nothing will happen to bhabhi now,' he added as he saw Shivsagar hesitate.

Shivsagar had never even boiled water in his life, let alone made tea. His hands fumbled as he boiled the water and then went hunting for the tea—god knows where Parvati kept it! He burned his fingers as he poured it into two glasses and his eyes filled up with tears of self-pity. How helpless he was without Parvati, he realized. If she had died today, what would have happened to him? Parvati's eyes were still closed when he returned with the tea but her breathing had improved.

'Wait, you son of a bitch, I'll tell your wife everything when she comes round. I'll tell her what you did to her when we placed her on the floor!' Badri said naughtily and noisily slurped his tea.

'What did I do?' Shivsagar asked haughtily but his hollow cheeks had a suspicious pink tinge.

'Oh ho, so you don't know what you did, is it?' Badri went on, enjoying his friend's discomfiture. 'Aji, if I hadn't been here, I can tell you that you would have given the pootonwali a sixth son tonight!'

And thus the night that had begun so tragically ended with both the friends laughing at themselves as they remembered the past. They had several more rounds of tea, and slowly Shivsagar unbent his spine to relax.

'I'll be off now,' Badri said finally. 'Don't worry, Shibu, your wife has come back from the dead. Now, make up for all your past cruelty and spend your old age undoing the lapses of your youth. Make your old woman lie on a bed of flowers from now on and beg her to forgive you for the past.' And this is exactly what Shivsagar did from that day on. He made up for every hurt, every cruelty he had ever inflicted on Parvati. She had suddenly aged and was now so frail that she could not even move about without aid. Shivsagar helped her sit up in bed, lovingly sponged her face and then hovered around while she bathed. Then, he would feed her porridge made by him and ask her to forgive him with every morsel he fed her.

'You've forgiven me, haven't you, Parvati? If you don't then I know that even god won't,' he said to her.

Parvati watched him with her limpid eyes from the bed. Was this really her husband speaking or was this a dream? If this is a dream, then please god, she prayed, may I remain here in this bed forever listening to him. Her emotional exile from his life had ended, she thought in wonder, and now her every wish was his command. 'I went mad with anger that day, Parvati,' Shivsagar went on. 'Even in my wildest dreams I had never imagined that my own son would bring such shame to our family. Do you know his wife is a Christian girl? His friend wrote and informed me of this wonderful fact!'

'Why do you take it to heart?' she replied in her soft, serene way. 'This must have been His will. Our son must have done something terrible in his last birth.'

Shivsagar looked at his wife in astonishment—there was no regret, no anger in that fathomless gaze. What gave her this extraordinary serenity? Parvati's only regret now was that she was confined to bed and no longer capable of looking after her husband. It pained her to see him struggle to knead the dough and roll the chapattis for their meal. Let me die, she prayed, with my head in his lap and please protect him from any further pain the boys may inflict.

The next month, however, brought more bad news and their fourth son, a doctor, flew the coop. She had always known that doctors prefer to marry their own kind, but could he not have found a wife within their own community? He could have told his father, couldn't he? To make matters worse, they heard that his father-in-law was languishing in jail on some murder charge. Thank god, the two went off abroad soon after they were married. Now all that was left was Chutke. This time, thought Shivsagar grimly, I'll not be caught napping. His son was in the Academy in Mussoorie, undergoing training after clearing the civil services exam. Badri had already warned him: 'Just remember, brother, that Mussoorie is like a huge auction, like the cattle fair at Sonepur. Either the girls there themselves entice these young boys or their parents do it. And then, Chutke is the least worldly-wise of your sons. Remember that the frightened swimmer drowns easily. Take my advice, find him a girl of your choice and clinch the matter right away. They can get married after his training is over.'

Shivsagar followed this sage advice but, once more, fate cheated him. Sometimes, he thought ruefully, if you make sure that you have bought the best pitcher for your home, you discover there is a leak that you missed. This is what happened with Chutke. Chutke had always been the most timid of his sons. Brilliant, yes, but terrified of his father. If he ever came back with 99 marks out of 100 in his maths paper and Shivsagar roared, 'Why didn't you get 100 marks, Chutke?' the poor boy lost his voice in terror. This time, too, when he told Chutke sternly, 'I have found a match for you and you will get married this Baisakh,' Chutke said nothing. He didn't even ask, 'Who is she? Is she educated or will she walk around like Amma hidden behind a veil?' Shivsagar thought he had found the perfect girl for his son. She was fair, pretty, slender as a reed and educated in a convent. Badri's brother-in-law played the matchmaker and found out that her father was a high-ranking police officer who had taken premature retirement but still a man of a stately presence. On Shivsagar's request, he had hired a house in the neighbouring town and Shivsagar went there for the wedding. He felt he could not ask his new daughter-in-law's posh family to come to his humble village house. Deliberately, he did not invite the two sons he had disowned but even the two he invited failed to turn up. One wrote that he was unwell and the other said his wife was ill. 'I know what this illness is, Parvati,' he sighed. 'If they had come, I would have felt ten feet taller before Chutke's new family.'

Chutke's wife came once to the village and then never again. God knows how long ago that was—so long ago that now Chutke even had a touch of grey at his temples. He'd sent a photo of the family—his slender wife was now as round as a drum, yet Chutke wrote how she was forever ill. Every third year, like an exotic rose bush, she went for a trimming course, or a surgery. Her gall bladder, appendix and her uterus had meant three surgeries. Shivsagar Mishra had been only once to see his son's house. Chutke had just become a Collector.

'Didn't Amma come with you, Babuji?' his daughter-in-law asked him sweetly. Shivsagar felt if he listened to her honeyed voice for too long, his blood sugar would rise.

'No.'

'Why? Is she unwell?'

'It's just that I thought the old woman still goes around with her face veiled. She may not fit into your kind of life.'

Shivsagar knew how to aim his barbs. He did not say, 'Did you invite her? All you said was, Babuji, please come once to see my new home. What about the woman who kept you in her womb for nine months, son? Did she not merit a similar invitation?' But he did not say all this. He knew his bullet had reached its target as he watched his son flush. Chutke was cut to the quick—of course, Babuji was right. How could he have forgotten his simple, loving mother! Time was when he butted the others away like an antler for the privilege of snuggling into her soft belly. There were just two people who still terrified the Collector—his father and his wife. Suppose his hot-tempered

201

wife had insulted his mother? He dreaded to think of the furore his father would create.

Chutke's son, Anand, was studying in an English-medium school and his daughter in a convent. Shivsagar was most dissatisfied with what he made of their education. All he ever saw his grandson read were comics, with his mouth working round a gob of chewing gum.

'Arre, why do you have to chew cud all the time like some buffalo, huh?' he asked his grandson one day. The boy did not even look up from the comic that he was reading. Shivsagar sat at the breakfast table with Chutke and his wife, his temper slowly rising to boiling point as the boy repeatedly ignored his father's pleas to join them. Chutke was familiar with his father's anger and hoped he would not get up and slap the boy. But that is exactly what Shivsagar did. He gave a sound cuff to his grandson. How was he to understand that what he thought was a deliberate deafness is the hallmark of a new generation of children. If they have a comic in their hands, you can go blue in the face before you get even a grunt in response. Chutke was a veteran of several cuffs from his father and never dared to question his authority. Not so his son.

'How dare you!' he yelled back. 'Who do you think you are to slap me?'

Faced with this brazen response, something snapped inside him and Shivsagar turned into the headmaster of a school who ruthlessly tanned disobedient students. 'I'll tell you who I am!' he said grimly, and started raining blows on the child. Chutke's wife pushed her chair and ran to snatch her son away from the hail of blows. She buried the child into her breast and turned to face him. 'You are an animal,' she spat at Shivsagar, 'we do not beat our children in this house!' Chutke sat with his head bowed, unable to say anything in defence of his wife or his father.

'I see that,' Shivsagar said with a sharp look at his son. 'This is probably why you have a son like him. This boy is in the seventh class but can't solve even a simple sum in arithmetic. He knows neither English nor Hindi. As for science, the less I say about that, the better. Tells me his father has given him a calculator so he doesn't need to learn his tables! One day, when it's too late to go back, you'll realize that all these things have rusted his brain. Shame on you,' he went on, 'that you have not taught him the elementary niceties of talking respectfully to his elders and politely to the servants. Yesterday, when your orderly reached his school late to fetch him do you know what he said to him?'

'What did I say?' interrupted the brat rudely, advancing like a spitting cat from under his mother's protective shield. Shivsagar felt if he could, the child would scratch his eyes out.

'I can't even bring my tongue to utter what you said,' he told the child. 'And when I offered to teach your pup,' he spat at his son, still sitting motionless at the breakfast table, 'your wife did not like it. I heard what she said to you in the veranda that evening, Chutke,' he went on, 'perhaps the poor thing did not see that I was reading the paper near the window and could hear every word.'

Chutke bent his head so low that it almost touched his plate. He wished he could duck out of sight under the table. But his father's voice carried on relentlessly, 'She was telling you, Your father's really got his claws into poor Anand. The minute the poor child returns from school, Babuji pounces on him. If he says he wants to go back to the village, please don't stop him. I'm warning you, if your father stays on any longer, he'll turn my poor Anand into a zombie.' Shivsagar turned to his daughter-in-law, 'You were right, bahu, perhaps I may turn your son into what I made my five sons: two administrators, a doctor, an engineer and a scientist. My students are now Commissioners and police officers. I may indeed turn your son into a zombie. I am fully aware now, bahu, that your house has no place for old men and women. Perhaps it's best if we, who your language describes as "oldies", are made to stand in a row and shot to death. If there is no old person in your world, there will be no trouble!'

With that, Shivsagar Mishra marched to his room, packed his belongings into his tin trunk and strode out of his son's house.

Chutke tried once or twice to make amends. He sent a draft for two thousand rupees once, another time one for five thousand. But each time, his letters were returned unopened. Shivsagar had liberated himself from the ties that bind parents to their children. His pension was sufficient for the two of them and he earned a little extra by giving tuitions to the village boys. Every evening, Badri and he set off for a walk and returned to find steaming cups of tea made by Parvati. It was pure ambrosia—the tea she made with tulsi, dried ginger powder, cardamoms and some special masalas that gave it a unique flavour. She added creamy milk from their cows to it and the two sipped it with bites of soft jaggery. The body felt revived after the first sip. Often Shivsagar would persuade his friend to share their evening meal and if it got late, Badri spent the night in the room on the rooftop. This was the oldest part of the house and the plaster had long fallen off the bricks. Badri and he had hoisted four sturdy bamboos to prop up the walls, so, all in all, Shivsagar was reasonably comfortable with his life.

Parvati, however, was shrinking by the day. Her face was white as a sheet and Shivsagar could not make out whether it was some terrible wasting disease or the indifference of their sons that was slowly eating away her insides. Every second person seemed to be suffering from cancer: did she have cancer, then?

He had spared no effort in her care, sat up nights holding her hand in his. But poor Shivsagar did not know that if you force-feed a starving man with rich food, it can kill him. He had starved Parvati all through their youth, so now if he was showering all his attention on her, was she capable of revival? Of course, she was as silent as always and never complained but he could see that even the most ordinary task exhausted her and she often sneaked off to lie down when she thought he was not looking.

Finally, Shivsagar could no longer bear it. He put aside his pride and, after ten long years, wrote a letter to his son. Shivsagar had heard that Delhi was considered the Mecca of officers, a Kumbh Mela of ministers. Chutke was now the Union Health Secretary and the destiny of the country's finest doctors was in his hands. Surely he would be able to save his dying mother, so he convinced a reluctant Parvati to go with him to Delhi. It was nearly a month since he had written to Chutke, yet there was no reply. Parvati's condition was deteriorating by the hour, so Shivsagar decided that it was futile to wait any longer.

'I was thinking, Badri,' he told his friend one day, 'that I shouldn't delay taking your bhabhi to Delhi. Chutke's written a number of letters saying I should bring her there.' Badri raised a disbelieving eyebrow as he looked at his friend. 'Achcha?' he replied, 'Chutke's invited you there? Then you must go, brother, but come back soon.'

Chutke used to love laddoos made by his mother, so even in her miserable condition, Parvati stayed up nights to make him all the snacks she remembered he liked—laddoos, besan ki namkeen, mathris and god knows what else. She filled huge canisters full of them to take with her. When they arrived, accompanied by countless bundles and canisters of snacks and their battered tin trunk, a Gurkha durban outside Chutke's bungalow refused to let them in. However, as soon as he was told who they were, he said, 'Come with me. You can wait in the "draaing room" because memsahib has gone out but she'll be back soon.'

For a long time, the two of them sat frightened and overwhelmed by their posh surroundings that had statues, carpets and huge chairs upholstered in velvet. Dwarfed by her son's prosperity, Parvati was reminded of their past—how cramped the past seemed in comparison to this expansive present! In those days, the only symbol of their comfort was the solitary armchair that Shivsagar had bought cheap at an auction. Its cane seat had worn out, so Parvati stuffed old cotton pulled from smelly old mattresses and stuffed it into a cushion to cover the hole in the seat. Her husband sprawled on it and, as long as he was in the house, this was his throne. But the minute he stepped out of the house, the boys would race each other to grab the seat of power. The victor would then spread his legs across it and declare, 'The throne now belongs to me!'

Today, each one of her sons was seated on an individual throne and no doubt they had all forgotten that childhood game. Only she endlessly nursed the memories of that lost age. She stole a glance at the stern visage of her husband: god knows what he was thinking. If she were in her own home, she would have served him three or four rounds of piping hot tea by now. Had they done the right thing by arriving unannounced like this? Suddenly their ears pricked at the sound of a car drawing up in the porch. Parvati quickly set down the bundle that she was holding tightly pressed to her breast so far and began to breathe quickly. Her husband took her trembling cold hand in his large, reassuring paw and looked at her as if he were telling her, don't worry, this is not some wild forest—it is our son's house. Yet at each approaching footfall, her heart went thump-thump in dread. She saw her son after a full ten years and was shocked to see the change. There was grey in his hair and moustache but how handsome he looked in a dark blue suit. Behind him was his wife, dark lipstick on her lips, short hair and a carefully made-up face. Her body was tightly encased in a short blouse and threatened to spill out at any moment. The minute Shivsagar saw the expression on his son's face, he knew he had made a hideous mistake.

'You didn't tell me anything, Babuji. I wish I had known you were planning to come,' he started, a slight irritation creeping into his voice.

'So shall we leave?' his father retorted.

'Of course not, how can you say such a thing?' he said quickly to cover his embarrassment. 'But if you had sent me a telegram, I would have sent a car to the station to pick you up.'

'Look at your mother's condition. I thought since you were such a big man now, you may be able to show her to some specialist here. And I did write but I don't think I got a reply,' Shivsagar could not help adding.

'You don't know what it's like here,' his son offered by way of an explanation. 'Sometimes it is almost midnight before I come home. And this is Delhi, Babuji, you have to set up appointments weeks in advance. Anyway, why don't you go to your room and freshen up? I'll see what I can do.'

'Where are the children, Chutke?' Parvati asked in a frightened voice, as if she had committed a crime by voicing this question. Chutke laughed loudly, and for a moment hope sprang in Parvati's heart as she remembered his laughter from the past. He always threw back his head when he did and his eyes would close on their own.

'They aren't children any more, Amma,' he replied. 'Smita is in Bombay working in a hotel and Anand is in Poona at the Film Institute.' Shivsagar's face closed ominously at this news.

'Oh, so he is going to become an entertainer, is he?' he asked in a tight voice.

'How can you say that, Babuji?' his son asked in an irritated voice.

The daughter-in-law did not say a single word to Parvati and as soon as she heard Shivsagar's comment, turned rudely and went into her room. Chutke followed her after an embarrassed pause.

After that, neither of them came to see them that day. A servant made their beds at night and asked, 'What would you like to eat, sir?'

'Nothing,' said Shivsagar, 'we have brought our own food with us.' Then he looked shamefacedly at Parvati, mutely apologizing to her for his earlier rudeness. He had spoilt her visit even before it had started.

And the two of them went to bed hungry.

The next morning, when Shivsagar opened his eyes, he saw Parvati lying with her hands on her chest, silently gazing at the ceiling. Her face was grey and pinched. Her body was like a skeleton with the skin stretched tightly on it and Shivsagar panicked.

'What is the matter, Parvati?' he asked her, lovingly stroking her cold forehead. It was wet, like grass when drenched with morning dew.

'Listen, please take me home,' she caught hold of his hand and pleaded, her eyes streaming with tears.

She had poured out her grief in that one sentence. He knew exactly how excited she was at the prospect of visiting her son's home, for Chutke had always been her favourite child. How many times she had told Badri before coming, 'I won't be back before a month. I'm going to tell Chutke that I want to see the parade on twenty-sixth January. We've spent almost the whole of December here, it'll be just a few more days.'

Then she had cooked every night to make the snacks that she had packed and brought with her. But no one had even bothered to ask what they were. Her daughter-in-law had cast one withering look at her battered tins and canisters, and Shivsagar had seen the contempt in her eyes. No matter how simple Parvati was, even she could not fail to notice that their arrival was most unwelcome. Chutke had stood near the door and spoken from behind the curtain before leaving for the office, 'I've told my PA to take care. He'll come here at about eleven tomorrow morning to take you both to the hospital. Tell Amma not to eat anything—all the tests have to be done on an empty stomach.'

Shivsagar was stunned at his callous son: his mother was dying and the swine did not have the time to take her to the hospital himself? At midnight, he awoke and found Parvati sitting in her bed, quietly sobbing with her head on her knees. He jumped out of bed and bent over her. 'What is it, Parvati? Are you in pain?' he asked.

'Take me home right away, please. I feel suffocated here,' she sobbed.

'All right, all right,' he patted her head. 'We'll leave tomorrow morning. Where will I find any transport at this hour of night?' he humoured her as if she were a child. 'Now, come on, lie down.' And like an obedient child, Parvati lay down once again, holding his hand so tight that he felt she was afraid he would run away if she did not hold him next to her. She had never behaved like this before, and a nameless fear took hold of his heart and squeezed the blood out of it. Was this because of the son and daughter-in-law's behaviour or did she have an intimation of her death? Her thin body was trembling and Shivsagar began to quake along with her. Sometimes she would say, 'They are coming, look!'

'Who's coming, Parvati? Where? There's no one here. Wait, I'll switch on the light,' he said and loosened his hand from her vice-like grip. In the dark, in an unknown room, he went fumbling around the walls and his head hit the door. A big lump formed in minutes but he still could not locate a switch. Finally, he tottered back to her bedside and lay next to her quiet, defeated and inert body.

Was this the end, then? He put his hand close to her nose—no, no, she was still breathing. She was alive.

'O god,' he prayed, 'if I have ever done any good in this life, then answer this last prayer. Don't let anything happen to her in this house. Let her reach home safely, let her die among the treasures she has buried there.'

Dawn broke and suddenly one crow cawed followed by a chorus of caw-caws. Two or three mongrels howled from the street and a brain-fever bird screamed against the sky as it flew across the lawn. The first ray of the sun fell on Parvati's white face and Shivsagar was reminded of the fleecy white autumn clouds of their village. She tried to smile as she saw his worried face bent over her but the pain turned it into a grimace. 'What is it, Parvati?' he asked. 'Are you feeling faint?'

He had to take his face next to her trembling lips to understand what she was trying to tell him, 'It is morning now. Take me home.'

'All right, you stay here. The rest of the house is asleep. If they wake up, they won't let us go. I'll go and get us some transport.' He was back with an autorickshaw within minutes. He told the driver to park outside the house so that its noisy engine wouldn't wake anyone. How he was going to take her back without a proper reservation or berth he did not care to think about. He carried out their luggage, then heaved his wife on his shoulders and sat holding her in an autorickshaw.

A train that was due to go to Saharanpur was standing in the yard. Shivsagar bought his tickets and sat in a compartment. He couldn't care where it was headed, just as long as it took him out of this cursed city. Every particle of dust seemed to him like a scorpion's sting and he was convinced that the minute they left it his Parvati would get better. He was right. As soon as the train started to move, she put her head on his lap and slept like a baby.

God knows how many times they changed trains, then sat through an interminable bus journey to reach home. It was night by the time they reached the village. Miraculously, Shivsagar's fear vanished as soon as he crossed his threshold. It seemed to him as if they had both escaped from hell and entered paradise. He would see how anyone could dare to snatch his wife from him on his home territory!

Early next morning, Badri arrived and Shivsagar went on and on about his son's magnificent house, the hospitality—'There are two cars in the porch, d'you know? One is official and the other his own. He has a huge house, but where does he have the time, poor boy, to enjoy all this? He had just returned after a trip to Japan with the prime minister, before that he had gone to Washington…they think the world of him…'

'Shut up, you idiot,' Badri interrupted rudely. 'Can one conceal a pregnancy from the midwife? I know what must have happened. I know all about ungrateful sons. What hurts me, brother, is that when it happened to me I came and told you all. And you? You thought you could fool me, huh?' Shivsagar bent his head in shame.

'You are right, Badri,' he admitted. 'I kept telling her all through the way that she was special, she was the woman our village calls pootonwali, a blessed mother of sons. But today I wish that she was childless. Do you remember that old rhyme we learnt in school, Badri?

Paanch poot Rama budiya ke…
Baki bacha na koi…

(Old woman Rama had five sons / And then there were none)
'Keep quiet,' Parvati's faint voice admonished him, 'don't you dare utter such inauspicious words. Why on earth should I wish to be childless?'

'I know, brother,' Badri went on, carefully stashing his half-smoked bidi behind his ear for later, 'this pain never lessens. The wounds your children inflict continue to hurt until you climb your pyre. They eat your insides hollow…' And, indeed, who knew better than Badri the depth of that pain? For the last ten years he had nursed his wounded heart for that was when he went over to visit his son in Bombay without any warning.

Badri had heard of Bombay and never dreamt that one day his son would live in that huge city of dreams. The son had married a girl of his own choice but, thankfully, she belonged to their own community. In the beginning, the son and his daughter-in-law would come down once in a while to visit the old man; then they stopped coming home. Nor did they ever invite him to leave his lonely life in the village and make his home with them. Badri slowly got used to living by himself. Then, one day, the son sent him a telegram to inform him of the birth of a grandson in Bombay. Badri went mad with joy— he ran to the local grocer's shop and quickly bought five rupees worth of batashas to distribute to his neighbours. A few women came over to sing the auspicious songs that are mandatory at the birth of a grandson.

'So when are you off, Badri Kakka?' they asked him. 'Why don't you call her here so we can see your grandson as well?'

'I will, I will,' Badri replied. 'Just let her come home from the hospital and recover her strength. I'll go over and see them both first.'

But that never happened and the child had celebrated two birthdays already. On his third birthday, Badri lovingly bought some hideous woollen clothes and caps in lurid colours to take as his offering for the child and left for Bombay. Thankfully, he had sent a wire to his son. Had he not done so, god knows where he would have landed in search of his grandson. The son and daughter-in-law had come to the station to receive him, but the minute they saw his rustic attire, their faces fell. Badri's dhoti, which he had washed himself, was yellow with age and distinctly dirty. His shapeless waistcoat was lined round the neck with grime and oil and his feet were stuffed into a pair of cheap shoes that squeaked as he walked. He got off the train, holding an old, battered tin trunk that had faint traces of roses and leaves painted in garish colours.

He reached his son's house and was stunned by its size and opulence. An ayah was walking the child on the lawn and Badri leapt forward to stuff a crushed five-rupee note into his grandson's palm. The ayah saw the note and turned her face away to hide her smirk—she had taken a hundred rupees from the memsahib for washing the baby's first nappy. Badri quickly made himself at home. He roamed around in his funny clothes and monkey cap and was all over the child, kissing him with his bristly face and smelly breath. Every morning, he took a neem stick from the bundle he had brought with him to chew as he cleaned his teeth, his caste thread looped over one ear. Then he stuffed his hand into his mouth to clean his tongue, making terrible sounds as he gargled and spat. Occasionally, he peed into the bushes at the edge of the lawn, oblivious to the horror of the neighbours. He ate in his room and polished off vast quantities of chapattis, saying, 'These Bombay vegetables don't have the flavour that our village vegetables do.'

'If they had the same flavour, god knows how many more

213

he'd put away,' the daughter-in-law said to her husband, when her cook informed her that the month's ration of flour was over in a week ever since sahib's father had come to town. Yet, she said nothing. Then Badri did something horrible. He had never tasted Coca-Cola in his life and knew that his son's kitchen had crates of it. Once in a while, he'd taken a sip from a glass but one day, when no one was around, he polished off almost the entire crate and fell asleep after many satisfied burps. That night, he peed in his bed.

'Sahib, tea,' the servant stood near his bed with a cup. Badri got up hurriedly and the servant saw the suspicious damp patch before he could cover it. He smirked as he saw the pool. Old men had accidents like this, but what would a man of twenty-five know of nature's cruel ways?

Embarrassed, he was just going to wash the sheet in the bathroom, when both his son and his wife came into the room, looking grim. 'Chhi, chhi, Babuji, have you come here to humiliate us in our own home? The servants are laughing at what you've done. We don't know how to face them.' He threw three hundred rupee notes on the table and said, 'I've told the driver—there is a train that leaves at ten, he'll put you on it.'

Badri Dube's face went bright red with anger. He said nothing as he threw the sheet on the floor, stuffed his belongings into whatever he could find—bags and bundles. Then, with his shoes loudly squeaking, he left never to return. He never left his village after that.

'Now I'll go straight from here to the ghat, understand brother?' he told his friend. 'Chander is dead and so are his wife and child. I am now a childless widower so today I welcome you and Parvati, the pootonwali, into my community.'

By the evening, Parvati seemed to improve. She asked for a bowl of milk, combed her hair, wiped her face with a wet towel, put a large bindi on her forehead and then turned to the two friends. 'Go,' she told them, 'both of you go and have a nice long walk like you always do. I'm fine.'

Shivsagar heaved a sigh of relief and went with Badri, as he always did on Tuesdays, to the Hanuman temple. All through the way the two friends cursed their ungrateful progeny and their daughters-in-law and felt lighter than they had done for days. Shivsagar undid the latch of his house and went in. Then froze in horror at what he saw: Parvati, dressed in her wedding finery, was lying peacefully on the floor. Her body was stone-cold.

Shivsagar sat motionless like a statue near her. His eyes were dry, and his lips grim as he gazed at her face unblinkingly. Badri felt as if his eyes were tethered to Parvati's face like the leash of a dog to a post.

'Cry, my friend,' he urged Shibu. 'Vomit out all that pain—otherwise you'll go mad, I tell you.'

But Shibu would not weep. He just went on gazing at his wife's inert body intently.

The night passed: the two friends sat silently, deep in their own thoughts and private grief.

At dawn, Badri stood up and said, 'Give me the addresses of the boys. We will have to inform them.'

'No,' thundered Shivsagar. 'I have no son. She was childless in her lifetime and that is how she will go from this world.'

The whole village collected as soon as the news of Parvati's death spread—the women touched her feet and called their married daughters and daughters-in-law to take a pinch of dust from Parvati's feet to place on their foreheads.

'Pootonwali Kaki has died a suhagan,' they said. 'What a fortunate way to go!'

It took less than an hour for the fire to consume her wasted body. Both the friends returned from the cremation, looking like two gamblers after a lost game of dice. There were still a few wilted flowers that had fallen from her bier at the threshold of the house.

And then it began to pelt outside, sheets of water swept down and, occasionally, a streak of lightning rent the sky. Suddenly they were shaken out of their seats by a sharp clap of thunder that seemed to have burst right over their heads. 'She's reached.' Shivsagar looked with red eyes for the first time into his friend's face.

'Who?' Badri asked, frightened by the mysterious smile that flitted briefly across his friend's face. 'Who has reached where?'

'Pootonwali. There,' said Shivsagar as he lifted his hand to the heavens.